No one Fears When Angry!

The Psychology of Confrontation

By
Jamie O'Keefe

Thanks to Mick & Jacky Neale & Mel for proof reading this book, also to my children Jamie, Ricky, Adam & Kirsty for being proud of me. Thanks also to my friends for being friends (you know who you are) and all my New Breed crowd, also to, L.V, Posh, Melissa and my little Kirsty for caring about me and making my heart smile.

Copyright Jamie O'Keefe 1999©

Published by

New Breed Publishing 2001

A CIP catalogue record for this book is available from the British Library

Printed and bound in Great Britain.

ISBN 0 9517567 9 6

Printed in March 2001 (1st edition)

Printed by
New Breed Publishing
Po box 511
Dagenham
Essex RM9 5DN

New Breed Publishing
Po Box 511
Dagenham
Essex RM9 5DN
England

Our Web site www.newbreedbooks.co.uk
Our email address books@newbreed.worldonline.co.uk

Front cover: Artwork by Maria Fetterhoff.
For artwork enquiries contact Maria direct via email at maria_cable@hotmail.com

Dedicated to the memory of my mother who gave her unconditional love to all regardless of how the rest of the world looked at you

I miss you dearly mum
Rest in Peace

4 Jan 1940 – 20 Sept 2000

About the Author

Jamie O'Keefe has spent 26 years studying, training and teaching the Fighting Arts. He presently holds the rank of 5th Dan black belt with the *'British Combat Association'* and *'The Self Defence Federation'* and is the chief instructor of his own *'New Breed system of Self Protection.'* Additionally he is also a former bouncer and has spent 15-years working the door. Whilst working as a doorman Jamie studied and gained his City & Guilds *'Further and adult education teachers certificate'* and then his Cert ed. *'Certificate in Education and training'* from Greenwich University. He is also an NVQ D32 D32 Assessor and *'Founder fellow of the Society of Martial Arts, (F.S.M.A.)'*

Jamie has written many articles for Martial Arts magazines and is a former columnist for *'Martial arts illustrated* and regular columnist with *Combat magazine.'* He has also been featured in *'Later'* and *'Front'* magazines. He has also appeared on BBC radio and on Television as an authority on Self-protection. In 1999 Jamie was inducted into the Martial Arts Hall of Fame for his 25 years dedication and promotion of the Martial Arts worldwide.

His favourite pastime is 'People Watching' and studying why people do what they do and has spent the best part of his life in contact with people displaying anger in some shape or form. He has now put pen to paper in the hope that he can put his own, and many other people's anger to rest.

This is his seventh book on Self Protection related subjects.

Jamie's other books are:

Dogs don't know kung fu - *A guide to female self-protection*
Old School-New School – *A bouncers training guide*
What makes tough guys tough – *How to become tougher*
Thugs, Mugs, and Violence – *Jamie's autobiography- so far!*
Pre-emptive strikes for winning fights – *How to win fights*
The Glory Boys – *The Mod gang culture of 1979*

CONTENTS

CONTENTS

Introduction

Anger! What a complex subject, yet one that undoubtedly affects us all in some shape or form throughout our lives, and sadly for some, it controls their lives.

After writing six books and countless articles for magazines. I came to realise that much of my writing was about the things that angered me most in today's society. I am not talking here about Sport – Politics or Religion, which are issues that I prefer not to discuss with anybody, because these subjects can break even the closest of relationships. I am talking more of the day to day things that bother us like traffic jams, domestic habits, irritating repeated actions and so on. There are a million and one little things that bother us and all contribute in some way to the emotional condition that we call 'Anger.'

A close friend of mine who incidentally happens to be a professional author himself, once said to me.

'Jamie, I can see in your writing that you are still angry about a lot of things. You are still writing about all the things in life that make you angry.'

He was right. I took a good look at myself and realised that I was still a very angry person, which I put down to the bad experiences that I have had in life. Evidence of this beams out in my autobiography *'Thugs, mugs and violence – the story so far!'* however the one thing that I have not yet explored is, why, when and what I, and many others like me, become angry at the simplest of things. Also to find out what can we do about it?

I decided to explore the emotion of anger in the hope that it will make me understand more about the subject myself and in turn I hope it will help others who read my book, to control, manage or eradicate their own personal anger; because anger has the ability to be a good or bad thing, depending on how you use it!

For the title of this book I give credit to a quote by the great Greek philosopher Aristotle (384-322 B.C.), student and disciple of Plato.

'Anger is caused by undeserved slight, fear by the perception of danger, but <u>no one fears when angry</u>' Aristotle.

What is Anger?

We all have our own definition and interpretation of what anger means to us so lets also take a look at how anger has been defined within the English dictionary and language.

Anger/ *extreme or passionate displeasure. To make angry.*
The Oxford popular English Dictionary

Anger/ *feeling which makes one want to fight or quarrel with somebody who has done or said something wrong or hurtful. He was filled with anger. Also – cause somebody to have this feeling by one's behaviour or words. My explanation only angered him more.*
Collins Junior Dictionary

Anger/ *a strong passion or emotion exited by injury.*
Collins National Dictionary

Anger/ *A violent passion, excited by real or supported injury*
The Cambridge English Dictionary

Well that's the wordsworth look at Anger but individuals living in the real world may describe anger differently!

Anger/ *it's when somebody really pisses me off.*

Anger/ *it's when somebody cuts me up in the car.*

Anger/ *it's when the checkout girl operates to slowly.*

Anger/ .... What's your way of describing it? What does anger mean to you?

The Law on Anger

There is no law to stop others or us from being angry. It's a secondary emotion, which we all have that can get us into, or out of, a lot of trouble, according to what we understand about it and how we use it. However the law of the land does come into play when the feeling of anger converts into spoken words or by our physical actions that may be seen as being threatening.

The law states that if someone makes you fear for your safety, they are guilty of 'Common Assault.' This can be caused even if they have not physically touched you. Making you *'fear for your safety'* is a breach of law.

'The law states that if the antagonist is aggressive and moving forward, and you fear for your safety, you can legally, pre-emptively strike the first blow in self defence.'

Now this is all based on the fact that somebody is being 'angry' with 'you' and that you genuinely fear for your safety, leading you to believe that you are going to come to some harm.

So the key words within that sentence are 'aggressive' and 'fear' which are both connected if you are on the receiving end of an angry person.

It is important that you understand the link between 'fearing for your safety' and someone displaying anger towards you. Although this is not a book about the physical aspects of protecting yourself if faced with an aggressive person, you must still bear this possibility in mind if you are going to fully understand the dangers of anger within confrontation, whether you are on the receiving or giving end, of anger and aggression.

If you are on the receiving end, you will now understand what the law allows you to do in order to stay safe. However if it is 'you' that are the angry one displaying aggressive behaviour towards another; you may want to rethink the consequences of your actions, because these bursts may leave you physically harmed within the boundaries of law, if your actions have breached the law by making someone 'fear for their safety.'

For example, under normal circumstances you may be the type of person that jumps out of your car displaying aggressive body language to vent your anger at somebody's poor driving. However if that person punched you on the jaw in response to you making them fear for their safety, they could actually claim that;

'You were moving towards them in an aggressive manner, making them fear for their safety, so they reacted by legally, pre-emptively striking the first blow in self defence'... See what I mean!

However normally you would see the scenario something like this:

You get out your car because you are angry at what they have done. They then hit you for no apparent reason and you naturally assume that they have broken the law with their physical assault on you... Well it's not as clear-cut as that if you take a closer look at what's really going on.

Can you see why it's so important to understand anger and aggressive behaviour within others and ourselves.
I fully understand the concept of 'fearing for my safety' when somebody is displaying anger towards me, which is why I will not respond to most situations by returning a display of anger. Regardless of the temptation to do so or how angry I may feel inside.

I want to make sure that if I am 'forced' to hit somebody, it will be in order to prevent them from further breaking the law, by stopping them converting their aggressive behaviour into physical application. I want to be able to control my own anger, by hiding it away, so that I can 'claim' to have feared for my own safety, justifying why I have had to protect myself.

All physical confrontations involve the emotion of anger but its how you recognise and use the outward display of anger within your own body language that will make the difference as to which one of you acted within the boundaries of the law.

All anger does not stem around the area of self-protection but most scenarios can lead to this or some level of criminal damage. So we cannot ignore the threat of violence from being discussed within this book.

Do You Have Anger?

As if I even need to ask this question!
We have all experienced anger in some shape or
form, but as we mature we seem to be more
capable of controlling, managing, hiding or
stopping our anger than we were able to as
children. But this also means that being able to
control, hide, stop or manage our anger that we
have to admit that we still have anger in the first
place. Also, not all of us improve with maturity!
There are some rare individuals in this world that
never appear to be angry but this does not mean
that they don't get angry, it just means that we
don't see it because it is cleverly disguised or we are blind to it.

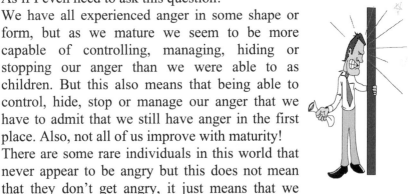

In many of us though, anger is something that we cannot hide or
disguise because it is written all over our face as an uncontrollable
expression for all to see. Just take a look at someone that has just
suffered an injustice towards them and you will see what I mean.
Some people will never directly admit that they are angry with you
after you have upset them. Even if you ask them outright *'Are you
angry with me?'* you may get a short blunt unconvincing answer
'No!' or *'What makes you think that?'*
However as hard as someone may try, it is very hard to disguise
'true' anger. The facial muscles will not allow us to.
So the answer to my question 'Do you have anger?' is definitely yes!
It may not be anger with another person caused by a confrontation, it

might be at the neighbours cat who happily
deposits the remains of yesterday's digested
dinner on your lovely flowerbed, or it could
be at the paper boy who always tears the
magazine as he pushes it through your
letterbox in a hurry, or the milkman who

continuously leaves your front gate open allowing it to swing back
and forth annoying you. Lets face it, there are dozens of things that
annoy you and continue to add small deposits of anger into your
mental proverbial 'anger bank.'

Switching Anger On

Some people actually want to be as angry as possible for certain situations. For example in 1993 for a TV documentary about prize fighting, the late Lenny McLean, Bare knuckle prize-fighter, and author of 'The Guv'nor' said, when asked about how he manages to switch on and psyche up for a fight, he replied,

'Hate, you must hate from head to toe, you must imagine that the person that you are about to fight, has raped your wife, interfered with your kids, you must hate that person more than you have ever hated in your life'

Think about this method of making yourself angry! If you actually convinced yourself that this fact was true of the person in front of you, or someone that you disliked. How would you feel inside?

For most of us, switching anger 'on' does not appear to be a problem when certain situations or conditions arise, but if you take a closer look you will realise that it is a very big problem because in most cases, it is not 'you' who is switching your anger on, it is somebody or something else that is switching it on for you, maybe even without their knowledge, but its certainly without 'your' consent. You don't really have any say in it, do you? They turn you on like a tap. They are the person in control; calling the shots and you are the one with no control over what is happening to you. *This is probably one of the most important things that you will learn from this book!*

When you look at it from this perspective you can see that other people having the ability to switch your anger on like a tap can be a real burden in its mildest form, going on to the other end of the scale, which could be dangerous towards you.

Our children, partners, and work colleagues are experts at doing this to you, but to be honest most of the time they really don't realise that they are having this effect on you. However, on the other hand some do and that's when you really need to be aware of what's happening so you can stay in control of the situation.

I have done this many times with ex-partners when they have done something that had annoyed me.

It may be something as silly as putting my paperwork away whilst she was tidying up leaving me unable to locate some notes or a telephone number that I need.

The reality of this is that a totally innocent act has angered me, so in turn I would seek revenge and do a few things that I know would 'switch on' her anger. For instance filling up the electric kettle to its maximum capacity and boiling it just to make one cup of tea. Something that I know infuriated her because it uses up two or three times the amount of electricity to boil the water. My purpose of doing this is to make her angry and believe me, it works. I wanted her to feel my anger, and suffer for moving my paperwork.

It's so petty and childish acting in this way and it embarrasses me to even write about it, but for the purpose of this book I have to explain certain things from my own experiences in order to help you to recognise and admit that you are probably doing the self same thing or something similar.

Anyway, getting back to me switching on my former partner's anger. She didn't know that I was angry about my missing paperwork, all she could see was me being wasteful by boiling the full kettle for just one cup of tea, and because its something we have spoken about in the past, she saw me as doing this deliberately to annoy her for no apparent reason. In turn, she decided to switch me 'on,' inducing my anger by doing something that she knows infuriates me and this goes on until we end up clashing with a verbal war.

This example of *'passive-aggressive behaviour'* being used to switch each other's anger on, is commonplace in almost all relationships. It's an indirect way of getting back at people without actually confronting them head on, or telling them why you are really angry.

This can be best described as *unexpressed anger*. Unfortunately though in some cases, this can also develop further onto a verbal assault, which for some, may progress onto physical violence. (*Not in my case I must add*)

So as you can see, other people switching you on at their leisure needs to be recognised and dealt with before it escalates. It's a bit like playing a game at which you are always losing at until you are given a few tips and pointers on how to improve your performance.

There are occasions when people have full intentions of switching your anger on because they want you to act in a certain way towards another person that 'they' do not like. Talking behind people's backs, backstabbing and shit stirring are all common phrases that are normally associated to this scenario. These type of people are always eager to freely put others down, criticising everything that they do. They are normally unfriendly, hostile, unsociable, cynical people that have not yet found a way to constructively express their own anger about someone else, hoping that they can prompt you to do it for them.
Keep a good look out for these type of people because they can be very dangerous with their loose tongues. Oh! And don't share any of your secrets with them.
Have you ever heard any of these sentences?

'I heard that your ex is telling everyone that you are a slut because you......'

'Sally said that she can do your job a thousand times better than you, and the only reason that you got the job was because...'

'That guy who works in the chip shop said that the reason you lost your job was because......'

'The trouble with your mother is...'
All common sentences that you hear time and time again in all shapes and forms, but all have the effect of switching your anger on.
Sometimes we find that our anger is switched on for us at an appropriate time and are thankful for this, like when a mother suddenly sees her child being led away by the hand of a total stranger, and her anger enables her to unleash a verbal and physical assault that would not normally be within her characteristics or capabilities.

A very similar thing happened to someone I know, whilst she was out walking her dog. An irresponsible owner allowed her boxer dog to roam free and viciously attack this person's dog.

Well! This caused the victim owner to release a verbal onslaught, advising the boxer dog's owner about being a 'irresponsible' owner. I think much of the advice given in her angry rage began with the letter 'F', again something very out of character for her but something brought on by anger.

How about the angry young lad (me) who stood up to the gang of bullies in order to protect his little sister who they taunted, making her fear for her safety. There are many similar true-life tales where people do not fear for themselves when angry.
A certain amount of anger is necessary to aid us in our survival; it is a natural response when we are in need to protect ourselves.
The possibility of others whom we care for coming to harm or actually being harmed does tend to instantly switch our anger on.
For some people though there are times when we could do with our anger being switched on, but it's just not happening because of our passive nature. We know that we are capable of being very angry because there are things that we have been angry about in the past, so how do we switch ourselves on, as and when we need it, in the same way that others are able to switch us on?

Well its certainly not easy – but it is possible.

You may well say to yourself,

'But I don't want to be angry, why should I want to switch my anger on, what use it that ability to me?'

Well my rationale for suggesting that you may one day need to be able to switch your anger on, is for the simple fact that it could save your life.
I have been actively involved in the teaching and study of self-protection for many years now, and have seen literally hundreds of

situations where individuals have been in confrontations with the ability to protect themselves, but fear has stopped them from sticking up from themselves.

Yet on the other hand I have seen other people with no capabilities or knowledge on how to protect themselves who were so angry by the situation at hand, that the anger overrides their fear and they successfully warded off the other party, whereas normally, this would not have been possible for them.

Prize-fighter Roy 'Pretty boy' Shaw creatively described his anger in his brilliant book 'Prettyboy' as being switched on when once pushed to far whilst serving in the army:

Roy said:

'He pushed his luck too far. I felt the adrenaline rush. It flared up inside me, starting at my feet, and surged throughout my body making me feel ten times stronger. It was an anger so uncontrollable, it erupted in violence.'

It's situations like this where I feel that the phrase *'No-one fears when angry'* was meant for.

When true uncontrollable anger is present, it leaves behind, and wipes out any fear that you have. That's my theory anyway!

I am certainly not implying that Roy Shaw was feeling fear, rather I am saying that there are some people that do naturally feel fear, who manage to overcome this negative response when they are overpowered by true uncontrollable anger.

So if you are in a situation where you are in fear of your safety and you do not like that feeling, you must find a way to rid yourself of this gut wrenching pain. One way that I am convinced of doing this is to make yourself uncontrollably angry. So how can we achieve this?

How many times have you said to someone?

'I just feel so angry, I can't control myself'

Or,

'He has made me so angry that I could......'.

That's the type of anger that I'm talking about, true uncontrollable anger, anger that does not allow you to falsely smile, anger that tenses up your muscles and joints, anger that makes you grind your teeth, and so on.

I can remember back to when my father died a few years back and I went to the hospital to collect his belongings. The night before he passed away I left him £30 to get through the next few days to buy magazines and snacks from the hospital mobile shop. I did not expect him to die at that moment in time. Sadly, he died in the early hours of the following morning, so did not have a chance to use any of the money, however when I signed and collected his personal possessions there was no money. The money itself meant nothing to me but the fact that somebody had robbed him around the time of his death switched on an uncontrollable anger, one that I could not begin to describe. Everybody who had any form of contact with him around this time was on my anger list.

This stupidly even included members of my own family, other patients, and other relatives along with all the hospital staff from porter to doctor. Anger can play some pretty bad games with your mind.

Parents experience this type of anger when they see their child being hit or picked on by another child. Their anger becomes explosive.

I remember once driving past my son's school and seeing him being beaten up by another child whilst the adults on playground duty were chatting away, totally oblivious as to what was going on right next to them. My initial anger that was switched on by seeing my son getting hurt, swiftly diverted over towards the adults who were displaying gross incompetence within their duties by not looking out for my son's welfare.

I was out of the car and angrily expressing my feeling towards them with no thought whatsoever as to any consequences. My actions were totally irresponsible, unprofessional and wrong, but anger took over any passive, logical format of verbal dialogue towards the adults on playground duty. That again is uncontrollable anger.

Wouldn't it be wonderful if we could shuffle our anger switches about a little so that they were switched off in scenarios like my example of the school, but switched on when confronted with a bully?
Well I think we can do this with a little thought and practice.

So lets try switching yours on now, be it only in the mind!
Here are some ideas to get you moving in the right direction.

Think of the worst thing that has ever happened to you in your life; like the bank that repossessed your home, the company that made you redundant, the partner that cheated on you, the friend that betrayed you, the person that robbed you of your savings, the person that hurt your child, the person who sexually assaulted you, the person that belittled you for a cheap laugh, The person that dumped you after sleeping with you, etc. These are all things that may have a similar bitter taste to something that may have happened to you which makes you feel uncomfortable. But are you really feeling <u>uncontrollable</u> anger? I doubt it; you are probably feeling bitterness and a bit of anger but its not uncontrollable. The reason is that we partly get over things; time does heal to a certain extent but the main thing here is that you cannot today, feel the same degree of anger that you felt at the time of an incident. The anger lessens as time goes by; even if it is only by a fraction of a degree, never a less, the amount of anger that you once felt has lessened.

What you need to do is to be able to feel 100% fresh true uncontrollable anger today, right now as if something has actually happened to you. It's not an easy task but it's got to be better than not being able to override your feeling of fear at all, at a time if ever needed. Most of our anger is our inner thoughts going to work and magnifying an incident that upset us some time ago. Most of the time our anger is not brought on by something that is happening right now, rather it's about something in the past, be it hours, days, weeks, months or years. The longer that we harbour it (Anger), the more we begin to add more and more false beliefs until we have blown the situation all out of proportion.

21

Eventually the anger is replaced by hate. This is not true all the time but can be for most of our false beliefs created by our original incident. So as anger transcends from its original state to hate, we find that our original feeling of anger has almost dissolved away and will do so even more over time. So when you think about how you feel about a situation or person, have a good think as to whether you are really feeling anger, or if it has changed into a different emotion altogether like bitterness or hate.

What I am trying to display here is the fact that if I ask you to think about something that has made you angry in the past so that you can feel that sensation of anger right now, you are unlikely to experience that same feeling after a period of time has passed.

If you want to feel anger right now you are going to have to create something right now, today that will anger you, it will be a fresh virtual experience, which plays on false beliefs.

To do this you are going to try to have a fresh experience within your own mind. Not one that you have been angry about before which has mellowed out over time. It has to be so new that it feels real. Almost like virtual reality. Remember again what I said about anger 'its all in the mind' regardless of what actually put it there in the first place.

Lets dream:

Now, imagine watching your own funeral, look at the faces of your children (if applicable), your partner, the faces of your parents, the faces of your friends all sobbing and suffering.

All these lives will be changed in some way via the loss of your life. Most of their lives will be re organised in some way because you are no longer around.

Now imagine the person that you most despise in life, which may be your current partner's ex, your own ex, a former friend, an enemy, etc who is also standing there laughing, prodding and poking your family members, imagine that person now forcing your current partner, child or parents to have sex with them and their friends in front of your children (if applicable) and family, whilst at the same time repeatedly prodding a table fork into the faces of your children causing them to suffer whilst their friends are stubbing out lighted cigarettes onto the skin of your other family members. The children are painfully suffering and begging for mercy along with your partner. Now add to this the thought of this person tying these family members to the bumper of a car then slowly driving along dragging them along whilst they are screaming out in pain. You look into the car and see your former employer, the one that always hated you, shaking and spitting in the face of your Grandmother, violently telling her what a waster you were, in front of your parents who are also bound and gagged screaming in pain from their skin being slowly peeled from their body with pliers by that school bully that has always haunted you. All this was caused in some way and made to happen by the person in front of you now, who if this was real, could receive your full expression of true uncontrollable anger.

This is the kind of thing that you will have to create in your head if you are going to be able to switch that anger on. Horrendous and horrific all these things seem, and sick and twisted as you may think that my mind is even thinking about these scenarios. These sick visions were not created in my mind; they were all taken from actual true-life cases from others with sick minds and have been added together for the purpose of this exercise. I think that the above-created scenario will certainly set you along the path of understanding how to switch on your own anger. If you put your mind to it, you will be able to think of some of the most horrific things that can happen to you and others including rape, torture and murder. The mere fact that you are able to think of some really grotesque things just goes to show that other people are also capable of these thoughts and some actually enjoy putting these thoughts into practice.

Doesn't that make you feel angry?

Once again, the strange thing about this is that prior to thinking of all these bad thoughts, the fear you would normally feel when confronted by this person would gone. You are hyped up, tensed up and ready to unleash your anger at anyone that even slightly gets in your face.

You do not feel fear when you are truly angry. Your fear will not completely go but their will be a few brief moments at least that fear will seem non existent whilst you are angry.

Some of us will not need to go to the extreme lengths of the ugly visions that I have suggested here. For many of us the mere offensive remark made about our parents or children can send the anger thermometer racing to the top.

A word of warning here! These ugly visions can sometimes partly, subconsciously, convince you that something that you have scripted in your head is actually true. This is something that has actually happened to me in the past on many occasions when my mind has been working along these lines. I have gone over something in my head, something that is untrue and convinced myself that it has actually happened.

This resulted in me genuinely becoming suspicious about people and former partners over situations that never existed! You could label it as unreasonable jealousy; which is probably why I am not able to hold a relationship together for longer than 5 minutes.

One former partner had become so used to my unreasonable behaviour at times that she would say to me,

'Been hearing little voices again have you?'

It would drive me crazy when something so stupid became imbedded into my head for reasons that I do not know, and 'the little voices' went to work, stirring things up for me.

There is even the danger of believing something so badly that you actually force circumstances to make it happen, without realising that you are doing so. I'm sure I'm also guilty of this one!

There is a saying that goes,

'It is done unto us as we believe'

So make sure that you are able to distinguish between a mind game that you are playing, in order to switch your anger on when its needed, from another much more serious condition which can be loosely defined as 'Paranoia' which became my demon.

I know two people who have dependency on drugs and alcohol who both create this paranoia world within themselves and believe their own creation that they put inside their own head so much, that, they act out the results of their beliefs in the real world, truly believing that other people are out to get them. This is a very dangerous condition to be in for all involved. For all you know, right now you could be the living nightmare that someone else has created within their own mind about you. It makes you think, doesn't it!

'As we think in our heart, so are we.' -- Proverb

Switching Anger Off

This can be as important if not 'more' important than switching anger on. Especially if it's your own anger that you are talking about.

People that cannot control or switch off their anger can get themselves into lots of trouble and in some cases end up with life imprisonment or in some countries, sentenced to death.

Even those people that have found a method or way to suppress or control their anger, believing that they have switched it off, may only really be sweeping it under the carpet out of sight, but lift the carpet and the same anger is still there.

I think the most important thing here (obviously), is to actually prevent things happening in the first place, which you know are going to make you angry, or deal with things that have already happened by reacting in a different way to how you have in the past. Some things though, cannot be prevented from happening.

If you take a look at someone close to you, be it a partner, friend, or relative; you will know exactly how they are going to react if they are angry with you. Some avoid being in the same room, others go and do, or redo the task that they expected you to do competently, and others will bang around and sulk. Whatever it is that they do, it will be predictable and is their way of showing anger. It is their way of reacting through habit. Now if you were to advise them on a different approach to showing that they were angry with you, such as a change in their habit, how would you prefer them to respond to anger in order to let you know that something is wrong?

To write you a letter explaining how they feel?

To call in an independent person to sort the problem out?

To fight with you?

To simply talk to you?

Well, the same also applies to other people that see you being angry. You will give off the same display of habit related anger and body language, which you have always done when letting off some steam.

You may sulk in the same manner as you have always done, or you might be a door slammer etc.

Now think about ways, which you could change the way you act, or maybe apply some of the things, that you have suggested that other people should use to change their anger related habitual behaviour.

Most of life's problems can be solved by reacting differently to them....I said 'most' <u>but not all</u>!

Some of life's problems are inescapable which can anger us even more when we cannot find a solution, reason being that we grow to believe that there 'is a solution to every problem' and when we cannot find that solution, because there isn't one, it frustrates us even more.

What we need to do is change our thinking. Instead of always searching for a solution to a problem, which can result in disappointment, if the solution does not appear, we should focus our mind on how best we can handle and face the problem. This way we will not feel so let down by our inability to solve our anger, instead we will be looking at ways to handle it and face up to whatever it is that has annoyed us.

Another reason that you may want to explore the idea of switching anger off - is if you are in a confrontation where another person is angry with you. Finding ways to defuse someone's anger could save you from an argument or it developing into a situation of physical violence.

For the macho guys who find it a hard task to admit that they would ever want to try and defuse someone's anger, rather than beating their brains in, I will use a different approach.

Imagine being faced with the Hounds of Baskerville, A Werewolf, or a rabid Rottwieller, you will now be able to allow yourself to think about defusing a situation of aggressive confrontation, rather than the usual tough guy response.

Life's problems are not all solved by who is the best fighter, because *'anybody can do anybody'* when it really comes down to it. You just have to find a way: and one-way is definitely by switching anger off, be it yours or theirs.

Anger Triggers

Imagine that your body is a gun and your bullets are your clenched fists or angry words, which can be fired when a trigger is pulled. Another person's words or actions can act as 'that trigger' which fires your bullets off. Wow! This means that you can be controlled by someone else like a puppet on a string. Not a good situation to be in. Especially if you are ignorant to the fact that somebody else is in control of your actions. It's bad enough when you find that somebody is setting off your anger trigger, but it can be even worse if you are setting off theirs, putting yourself in danger. This is definitely a two way street!

I knew a girl who was newly married and madly in love with her husband, however she was not so fond of the physical violence that he dished out to her when they were arguing.
On speaking to the pair of them individually in the capacity of a friend, it was quite clear what was happening.
Firstly before I explain, I wish to make it clear that I do not find the use of domestic violence acceptable in any shape or form and I would have lost no sleep at all if the male concerned had been put in prison for his actions.
If men want to be tough guys then they should try it against other men who would be a fairer physical match and hopefully they will be repaid for the abuse they have handed out to women. Please don't take this last sentence in a sexist sense – lets just stay in the real world for a while!

Now, getting back to the story. I tried to see why the violence was occurring and how it could have been stopped.
It seemed that both parties were acting out their anger with each other in the way that they were both accustomed to doing with their previous partners and also through habit.
He was used to storming off to 'walk off' his anger or would bang his fists and let his partner know that if she didn't back down and shut up, violence could be the next option.

This was his anger-related habit and way of dealing with problems in a way that he had done over the previous years with previous partners.

She on the other hand was used to having a fully blown row because she was very educated and liked to use her knowledge of matters to win, plus she also would also not back down, continuing the argument until she had won or had been proved to be wrong. This was the way that she was used to doing things within her previous relationships through habit. She was also not shy of throwing out the odd jab or cross herself.

Now comes the problem and trigger.

When an argument developed, she would not allow him to walk away to cool off, her reason being that the problem would still exist when he returned and it would have to still be dealt with, so even if he did manage to escape for a while, he would still have to face the music on his return.
She would block his path, taunting him, scream at him and would even hit him.
Like a cornered animal with no way out, his trigger was pulled to which he responded with a verbal and physical beating until she was no longer able to retaliate. He had released his anger. Although she could not match him physically pound for pound, she paid him back eventually by leaving him patching up a broken heart, however she remained in contact via telephone hundreds of miles away, where she was safe and he went through a mental torture that he could never have conceived. I know her intentions were never to seek revenge on him, but I still witnessed him go from a big strong man into a sobbing drunken empty shell. I listened to his pain every time that I spoke to him after they split up and saw how she had taken him to pieces bit by bit even though this was unintentional. There's a way to do everybody, no matter how big or tough they may be and she found her way to deal with him.
We spoke about all that had happened between them and he realised that he had destroyed his marriage via his use of physical violence.

He basically was a jealous bully.
He said to me,

'If only she let me get out of the building to walk around and cool off, she was like a trigger setting me off every time she blocked my path and made me feel cornered.'

I think that if they were prepared to sit down and find another way to deal with the anger, avoiding a head on collision, then maybe, just maybe, things would have worked out for them.

I really wished their marriage had worked for them however I hasten to add that I truly believe that he would have eventually beaten her to death one day or she would have killed him. She did the right thing in ending their marriage, for both their sakes. I have no sympathy for him for the way in which he acted and I'm sure that he will regret it for the rest of his life. He is still walking around a very bitter and angry man, still using violence on others weaker than him and is gradually loosing every person that ever cared for him. I personally could not accept his behaviour within my social circle and gradually became distanced from him. I threw away a 20-year friendship because I was not able to accept his violent and offensive behaviour to others weaker than himself or to those that genuinely respected and helped him. I really hope that he can come through this and make a change within himself so that he can become a better person. Maybe, just maybe, this book will help. If he ever reads this book then he will recognise himself straight away and will be able to decide if he has now got a grip on his anger or if it still has a grip on him! What he will not be able to do though is change the past, we can only change the future!

Getting back to the situation between the couple, I asked each of them if they would like to contribute anything to my research on anger. Neither of them were aware of what the other had wrote. Here is his contribution.

'Jamie, I have finally put pen to paper with regards to the question of anger. I could go into films and Literature, but I'm sure you have covered this already so I will just give you my personal view on the subject. The thing I have found over the years is that I have two types of anger.

1. *If I bottle things up like I used to (which I'm glad to say I don't anymore) over a period of time, I would just explode. To me it's just like somebody with a clockwork toy, winding it up slowly until in the end something has to give. Also I find that the anger I have does not overcome any fear that I may have.*
2. *The next type of anger I have is the one that I fear most because it's very dangerous, however providing I keep the first one in check, I can control the second one.*

What usually happens is that within a normal conversation where we could be laughing or joking about, someone's actions or words which I normally would not take any notice of, would on this occasion would for some unknown reason- switch something on in my head. I would just click on and lose the plot completely. An example of this was that time I chased a guy I knew, through the woods whilst holding a big knife. I would definitely have killed him had I caught him and it was only the voice of my partner at the time that enabled me to switch off. Fear never came into this equation. Jamie, my only real fear is that the next time this happens, there will not be any voices present to disarm me.'

A year or so down the line I witnessed this type of anger get control of him again; which wiped out any fear that he had for his own safety and for the reaction to his actions. These senseless few seconds lost him more that he ever wanted or envisaged.

She wrote the following.
ANGER

Well, you Jamie have asked me, to think about anger, which is a bit weird, because, to me, anger is not a well thought out process. For I fear that too much reflection on the subject might deprive it from it's very meaning; I will try to give my views in an abrupt and impulsive way.

Personally, I do not really know what anger means, though I know what it is like; but like many people I do not admit I am angry: 'Are you angry?' 'No, I am not bloody angry' I reply with a resentful tone in the voice!

I know that anger is supposed to be one of the seven sins along with gluttony and lust, which I know as well.
For my part, I would say that anger is derived from 2 different mental processes:

-Bad anger comes from negative feelings like jealousy, envy, possessiveness (?), aggressiveness, frustration and so many more,....
-Good anger can be caused by a feeling of disgust: unfairness,...It is like a normal reaction to an unbearable situation.

Now, anger can take on several aspects, and god, do I know it!! The first one I can think of is violence in it's physical way, then you have nice little things like revolt, disgust, vengeance,..... I will not refer to each and every one of them, as I am personally concerned, I will pick out what suits me best.

Lots of people think I am an emotional and crazy person, though I look nice and normal.
Why that judgement? Just because I'm an extrovert and show my emotions.

Back to anger: to make things easier, I have made a little interview of myself, like psychiatrists do when they analyse you.

-A definition of anger:
Anger is, as far as I am concerned, what happens when your life is made unbearable by a little thing. I am usually tolerant, but anger comes without warning when somebody or something interferes with my well-being.
Anger is like fire: destructive, but purifying; If you do not get angry you may become resentful or frustrated which is worse.

-The release mechanism:
I can be angry if I feel concerned by a certain subject: for example, I cannot stand people hurting animals or defenceless human beings. It makes me feel very angry because the situation is unfair and like a super hero I interpose myself. It is like saying 'all right boys, if you want to attack somebody, try one who can fight back!!!'

Though I am not big, I have always been very lucky, maybe because I am a woman and people are surprised. I will always remember one guy who said 'she is crazy, she must have a gun to act like that.' Some friends even call me call me 'Tank girl', I personally think they watch too much TV. All this is due to anger; I just turn into someone else.

The second reason that comes to my mind is purely physical. If somebody is trying to hurt, to push or to touch me in a way I feel is inappropriate or aggressive, I cannot control anger, adrenaline, or myself or whatever you call it just comes out.
I am sorry Jamie, but even if someone with your capabilities, tried to beat me up, I would not be afraid.
Because not only anger has the ability to make you blind, it also makes you feel a lot stronger than what you really are. That is when it becomes really dangerous especially if you really wanted to beat me up!!

-What does it feel like?
Personally, I do not consider myself to be a nice girl anymore; I have become more like a psychopath. I do not care about people taking the piss out of me, but if I am touched in my physical integrity without giving them permission, then I am a raging bull. I am no longer afraid of the size, reputation or appearance of my opponent; anger switches my fear off and turns it into violence.
The process that leads to anger is always similar as far as I am concerned. First I ignore the disturbing element, then I start to get angry, so I speak out and give a warning, if it does not work I get angry for real. I am a civilised woman after all.

-The consequences:
It is generally a very loud argument, but it is great because it lets
steam out. I try to avoid a fight because I care about my looks!!
BUT....If I cannot express my anger, it leads me to frustration and it
might make me feel angry at people who do not deserve it, which I
would hate. Too many frustrated people pick on their kids or partners,
that is really unfair; and since I hate unfairness more than anything I
do not tend to be frustrated or resentful. So I have a go at what really
annoys me.

-The limits:
When I said I would not care about whom my opponent was, that was
a little lie. I have had physical fights with my sister, my father, my
stepfather, and my previous boyfriend, to which I resorted to using
violence successfully. I have kicked him in the belly, kicked him in the
head, hammered him in the corridor; head butted him and so on.... I
was only 17 at the time, and very angry. I was a right cow.

We all have taboos and mine are animals and kids, I could not harm
them. Some men would hit their wives but could not hit another
member of their family, or a friend for a mysterious and unconscious
reason. That is what leads me to:

-Anger and violence:
They are both linked, at least as far as I am concerned. Though I am
more likely to be verbally violent, I cannot help but physically fight if
something or somebody goes over my limits. I am a very angry girl,
maybe because I am not patient or I am too demanding, I do not go
around hitting people because I cannot afford it, but rather I make
this choice because I dislike violence.
But then, I like anger, it makes you feel alive. If nothing makes you
angry you are mentally dead. I am very suspicious of people who are
never angry; it may be the sign for something more dangerous. Then
again, it is my Latin side speaking and it also depends on sociological
factors (like parents influence, social class,...).

-The exception:

The only person that really made me angry and whom I could not reply to was my husband. He was himself a very angry man and he focused his violence and frustration on me. I soon became the reason for all his trouble and the cause of his anger. It was very unfair but as he would not let me argue without finding a reason to hit me, I became very angry, resentful and frustrated. I became so afraid of him that my anger was not enough to save me, instead, I learned patience and control. We have split now and I am still very angry at him, because I could not express this feeling, I am afraid it is trapped in me now.

-Good or bad?
The ambivalence of anger would take thousands of books to analyse, that is why I keep with my own feelings, I am conscious that I cannot mention every notion of anger. I am sorry I have been so approximate but to give a true impression of anger but I did not prepare my answers.
To conclude, I would say that what helps controlling your anger is expressing yourself, it might avoid violence. But I am not perfect and I have got no lesson to give. To me anger is like fear, it can be a motivation and help you to get out of a difficult situation. Anger needs to be controlled though because it can lead you into a lot of trouble.
I like being angry because I feel I am alive. Anger can make you achieve great things; it gives you a soul if you use it properly. But anger is only valuable if it is constructive, otherwise it turns into violence which is the antithesis of life.

This was her articulate reply to which I must add that you can see that she is quite capable of putting up an educated argument using accurate, logical information with underpinning knowledge. Also English is not her first language so she impressively translated her own reply to into English herself.

After reading her notes and thoughts on anger, maybe you feel differently about the way in which she confronted the problems between herself and her husband?

You may even feel that her anger was not really with him but more as a result of her bad memories of her teenage years. Then again, after reading his notes on anger you may think something quite different!

I don't really know the answer, I'm not their psychologist, I was their friend, however I am still of the belief that he should not have released his anger in the form of physical violence. I compared their relationship to that of late punk rock star Sid Vicious and his girlfriend Nancy. They both died as a result of their explosive anger with each other and the world, and both my friends admitted that they both firmly believed that their fate would follow a similar route had they remained together. She is now back in her own country and he has stayed in his homeland – England.

They can both now argue, fight, love and care about each other but with the safety net of a telephone and hundreds of miles between them. She is still very angry for all the torture that he put her through and he is angry with himself for messing up. His anger is still being unleashed, in the form of bullying and intimidation towards the people that he now comes into daily contact with. He is still in denial that he is a bully to those weaker than him.

It is such a shame that anger forces them to be apart.

There are many relationships just like these. I really don't understand why people stay in relationships when it involves violence and anger bullies. If at all, it would be more understandable if we expressed this type of behaviour against those that we don't like and not to those that we are supposed to love!

However most of us have been there and have stayed within this type of abusive relationship for a multitude of reasons, but in my opinion, no reason is good enough for any individual to allow violence to be used against them.

Recognising Anger in Yourself and Others

Psychics, Fortunetellers, astrologers, counsellors, friends, religious advisors, doctors, partners and the like are always at hand to tell us what our actions mean and what we are thinking. However when you think about it, you are the only one, and also, the most well informed about your deepest thoughts, which includes your own personal feelings, thoughts and beliefs. At times we all need to ask ourselves what we are really feeling like, in order to recognise our own true anger. Nobody can do this better than ourselves.

For most of us, our anger can be seen in the form of unhappiness caused by repressed anger. This in itself may be baggage that we have carried around for many years but we do not recognise it as such, because for some of us it goes as far back as our childhood. This state or condition may even seem usual or normal for us, which is another reason that we will not recognise the fact that we are holding anger, which is 'invisible' to ourselves. Anger can almost be like the Emperor's new clothes.

People and things outside of ourselves may not even be the thing that is making us angry. Something may be triggering our repressed anger, which is not the same thing as something causing our anger.

For example it is very hard to recognise what its like to 'become' fat if you have always been fat, or be a cockney if you have always been a cockney, a scouser if you've always been a scouser, a male if you have always been male, or without sight if you have always been unsighted; well the same thing applies to people that have always been angry. They may not recognise that they are actually angry because they do not know any difference. They have always been angry but it's been confined within themselves. You may call your anger something different just as a pair of trainers can be known by different people such as sneakers, training shoes, footgear, pumps, etc but to all intents and purposes they are still trainers.

Look at the body language of someone from a different country whose language you do not understand; when they are being aggressive you can see it, no matter what label they attach to their display or their mother tongue. Same applies to anger.

If you feel irritated about something or something is bothering you, you are still feeling anger. If you are disgusted at something or upset, you are still angry.

If you feel resentful or frustrated at something then you are still angry.

Do you get my point, call it a 'rose by any other name' but it still boils down to one thing-you are angry, so recognise it as such. Recognise that you are angry. Do not go into denial or brush aside your feeling of being annoyed as you 'not' being angry, because deep down you most probably are!

Impatience is another word for anger. Is this a feeling that you recognise? Are you impatient at

being put on hold by the telephone operator? Or are you really angry with the operator or the fact that your cheque payment has been lost in the post and as a result are about to be disconnected from the telephone service? Are you really irritated by the postman delivering your mail each day after you have left the home, or are you angry at your dog for chewing up your mail.

Are you angry because your latest diet hasn't worked as it had claimed it would or are you really angry at being overweight in the first place?

You must learn to recognise your anger before you begin to find ways in which to deal with it.

I get annoyed when other people let me down if I've expected them to complete a task for me. But am I really angry at them or am I angry at myself for not being able to, or not putting myself out to do the task myself?

I once went to America for a couple of weeks and asked a trusted friend to run my business for me so that books were sent out and customers were kept happy. I returned from my holiday to find a carrier bag full of cheques and orders but no books sent out! I lost a few of these orders due to cancellation and my promise to supply my books by return post and I also lost future orders from some people who expected a more efficient service. However I did not get angry with my friend for letting me down, rather I got angry with myself for making a promise to customers that I did not keep. Sure my friend did let me down, but what friend hasn't done the same to us at some time on some level.

Shit happens and people have more important things to do within their lives than try to make me successful. I understand this fact more than anyone and can recognise my own anger.

It is also important to recognise anger in others sometimes, even if they cannot recognise it themselves. It helps you to remain friends with someone that doesn't realise that they are venting their anger on you, although they may not recognise this fact.

I had a friend once who was hiring a hall to teach his subject. He had an agreement with a small group of people to hire out the hall on a weekly basis for which they would cover the rent. Prior to this I had given my friend the keys to my training centre so that he could teach his people at my place free of charge and build up his group along with making himself some money. He had the freedom to use my place day or night at no cost to himself, which I was quite happy about. Six months later my place closed for renovation and I needed somewhere to do some teaching for just one hour, once a month.

I asked my friend if I could now use his spare unused room at the same time that he himself was teaching so that it would not add any cost or inconvenience to him whatsoever. He kindly allowed me to use his room at no cost for the hour.

The second month came and one hour before his group were due to attend his class, he had a phone call saying that they had to cancel. My pal then panicked about covering the rent and called me to say that if I wanted to use his room that evening, I would have to pay him some rent, even though he had just had six months unlimited use of my gym for free!

How would you read and deal with this situation?

I recognised my friend's anger, which was being used towards me, as being the result of his true anger at the group that had let him down. He wasn't angry with me, he didn't really want to take any money from me, he was just angry. In fact I had taken him and his wife out for a meal only a few days earlier so I know that he was not really angry with me. I recognised the fact that he was angry about being let down by his group and I did not let that interfere with our future relationship as friends.

I spoke to him about this a few days later to try and get him to recognise his own anger and with whom he was really angry at. I think he understood how he misguided his anger at an innocent person, (me). We are still good friends to this day and both learnt a little more about how anger affects people and its possible effects on friendships.

Recognising anger in yourself and in others is a very important thing.

If your friend or colleague makes a comment about sport, politics or religion that you find uncomfortable. Have a good think about what it is that you are really pissed at. Is it really your friend's comment, or is it the bigger issue that you are angry about? If you are unhappy with your friend's remarks, you should be happy that you are in the position to challenge their views and set the record straight. It may even be the fact that your friend's comments are valid and that it is you that are wrong! What you must try to recognise is the fact that you are most probably really angry at something much bigger which you are not able to sort out.

You may not be in the position to take on the government, religious leaders etc, so in turn you take your anger out on the one person that has unknowingly set you anger alight.

I myself have blown a fuse in the past when I have heard people talking about the homeless as being lazy, not wanting a job, being dirty, begging and so on. I always seem to hear this from people that have comfortable lifestyles in comparison to the destitute people living on the streets. I see most homeless people, (not all), as being victims of circumstances who have lost some very important things in their life, which may be their job, home or family and as a result have had a nervous or mental breakdown, which has gradually put them out on the streets. They have lost the desire to help themselves and have become used to helplessness, which in turn holds them back from a better quality of life. So when I used to hear people bad mouthing the homeless it would make me so angry.

However I now recognise that I am really angry at the bigger issue of how society treat these people differently because of their personal circumstances. It is society or the government that I am really angry at and can now recognise this in myself. Prior to this I would end up in a full-scale argument with someone telling them how ignorant and offensive I found their remarks, and then go on to give them a hard time.

I now recognise my anger as it begins to pop up and swap it for sensible discussion and debate. I try now to not let my repressed anger trick me into reacting towards people in an aggressive way when it is not really them I am angry at. I also try to recognise anger in other people so that I can tell myself that their actions towards me are a knock on effect from something else that happened to them earlier.

Like the checkout girl that is throwing my food along the barcode scanner just that little bit to aggressively for my liking. She may be angry at the fact of not being given a break, or the previous customer was rude to her, or management telling her to work faster, who knows? All I know is that I do not want to take home cracked eggs and broken biscuits so I will deal with the situation. I would say something to the girl in a polite manner like,

'Could I help you pass these items through, because I do not want my shopping to get damaged as it did in another shop last week.'
Or in a humorous tone,
'You look like someone's upset you, hope you are not going to take it out on me, I'm one of the good guys.'
I could of course just have an argument with the girl and tell her what I think of her actions, but that's what we're trying to get away from, isn't it.

We are trying to recognise anger in others and ourselves so that we can have more control of situations and ourselves.

Many of us in relationships take out our anger on the people that are closest to us because we know we can partly get away with it and make up later on, whereas if we vented out anger at the person that really pissed us off I.e. our boss or work colleague, we could find ourselves without a job the next day.

I cannot count the number of times I lost jobs in my youth because people that I worked with had annoyed me in some way and I unleashed my anger on them. My problem was the same as most other people however I did not know how to manage my anger and did not recognise that I also carried the baggage of repressed anger, which I took from job to job, adding more weight to it as time went on. I didn't have a book like this on to help me understand myself. I preferred to knock somebody out and lose a week's wages rather than even attempt to control my anger at a 'Jobs worth bully foreman.'

I eventually found a way to combat my explosive anger with bullying foremen by becoming self-employed and my own boss. I had similar problems with bossy partners in relationships so I dealt with that one by becoming and staying single. Like I said! There are alternatives to anger which you can use until you come up with something better.

One thing that I must add here is that I am definitely not trying to put across the message that *'Anger is a bad vibe man!'* and that you should just turn the other cheek and forgive your fellow man for being angry at you! I'm not into all that spiritual bollocks!

I am a realist, living in a real world and anger can be a very serious matter, which must be dealt with in some way. We are not judging the quality of a cake in a village church hall; it may be that we are judging as to whether we are about to lose our life or not through someone being angry.

Dealing With Anger at Simple, Serious and Life Threatening Levels

I see anger at three different levels, that being, simple, serious, and life threatening. We could get technical and add many sub levels and extensions to these three if we wish, but I think that my three method of recognising anger are sufficient.

Lets break my three down into their individual units so that I can explain why I only bother with these three levels.

Simple Anger

In my opinion, simple anger is something that can be dealt with 'simply' whether it is your own anger or that of another person. To me simple means a situation where you are not at risk of harm and are not going to get physically hurt.

An example of this would be something like when you have heard somebody spreading malicious gossip about you or someone close to you. It makes you angry, however it is not something that puts you in immediate risk of physical harm, unless of course the gossip leads to someone else hearing and believing it, and wanting to break your legs. But generally, anger at a simple level can be defused in a simple manner through sensible debate or simply just by ignoring it. Some people find it much harder though to take an insult to their pride as something that they can deal with simply, however theoretically it can be dealt with quite easily. What you must not allow, is to let anger that 'can' be dealt with at a simple level, escalate onto the next stage, which is anger at a serious level.

You must find the way that works best for you to defuse this simple anger. If it is you that is angry at another person then do whatever it is that you have to do to get yourself out of that situation, be it locking yourself in a room and watching your favourite comedy video, going jogging, or even confronting the person that has made you angry, if you know you can do this without it progressing onto the serious level. There is no point in confronting someone if deep down you know that it could escalate into a situation that brings with it violence.

That may make you feel better for the moment, but this whole book is about dealing with anger in a positive way that will avoid violence, no matter how attractive a violent encounter may seem at times. Discussion can work as an exchange of knowledge and logical options, whereas an anger fuelled argument could just end up an exchange of ignorance.

If it is someone that is angry with you, then you are going to have to apply the same set of rules to enable 'you' to defuse their anger and drop it down a level, rather that let it rise up onto the serious level.

Serious Anger

Well this is where you are very likely to feel the result of anger physically, rather than just being hurt mentally. You are likely to feel physical pain as a minimum, which is likely to lead onto bruises, broken bones and open wounds. In other words, a good kicking could be on today's menu, if you do not defuse it and drop it down a level.

This situation is not good for you if you're on the receiving end and also not good for you if you are dishing it out testing fate with a prison sentence, so either way, you are going to have to deal with it.

My method here is to once again defuse the seriousness of this anger by doing all you can to drop it down a level. Think of any reason at all to get away from the person who you are about to hospitalise, or if they are going to do the self same to you, so that you make physical contact impossible. Then carry out the rest of the defusing over the phone, by letter, by friend, or even by email. I actually had an email 'row' with a former pal of mine which would have no doubt have got heavy and violent in some shape or form if we did argue face to face. We were both too stubborn to back down to each other and ended up parting company without any ugly violence. This way neither of us publicly lost face and could both go and tell our partners, friends etc about how we won the battle and all the other macho bullshit us males go through as part of our hard man ritual.

If you are really trying to get to grips with dealing with anger at all levels, then you are going to have to deal with matters that do seem alien or even cowardly to you, but that's life.

You cannot have all the good sensations and none of the bad if you are truly going to deal with the anger monster.

Life Threatening Anger

In my opinion, Life Threatening anger is something that may evolve onto something that is going to alter the quality of someone's life as they live it now. How we currently live our life now 'is our life', however if that is reduced in quality and forces us to drastically change how we live, then to me, that is life threatening.

My friend Martin would have laughed his head off years ago when we were kids at my suggestion of dealing with his own anger by backing off and finding another way to deal with a serious situation.

I have been side by side with him faced against 30+ guys who could still not make him back down. He is now serving life for the taking of a life in a situation of self-protection with situation that did not even involve him being angry!

Someone else I knew was the late Reg Kray (Kray Twins) who had also served 32 years for a similar offence until his own death, but his did involve the emotion of anger. Makes you think doesn't it, for a few moments of uncontrollable emotion, four lives are taken away. Two by death and two by prison sentence. It just isn't worth it.

I do apologise for the name drop again but I was chatting with prizefighter Roy Shaw the other day and we discussed how he deals with his anger at a serious level. He said that in his younger days he had nothing to lose but his pride; so would blow up at the simplest of situations regardless of the consequences.

Roy Shaw & Jamie O'Keefe

However now, many years later, he has fought his way to the top to become a very wealthy business man and knows that he has a lot to lose if he carries on fighting with every person that wants to make a name for themselves. He does not want to swap his millionaire lifestyle for that of an inmate. He's tried both and prefers the millionaire lifestyle, which is the deciding factor that helps him to control his anger.

A word of warning here for the brave hearted, don't misunderstand Roy's preference of lifestyle as being a sign of weakness, because he is still a man who will suffer liberties from no one! If he comes calling – hell's coming with him. Roy is the real McCoy.

So have a good think about the level of anger that you are faced with in any given situation. Habit may try and force you to automatically raise the level of anger, but if you really want to deal with the anger monster then you are going to have to learn, practice and be prepared to bring it down a level. It may just save your life or that of another person.

The Priest & the Thug

Who do you think would more likely make you 'fear for your safety' had you just cut them up in the car, a Priest or a Thug?

For most of us I think it would be the thug because we are more inclined to believe that the thug would react by using violence, whereas the priest would be more likely to smile and forgive you.

What are the chances of the reverse happening? The priest kicking off and the thug apologising? Not much chance I think! But sadly this conditioned thinking also affects our outlook and actions towards situations like this. After upsetting the thug and seeing him get out of the car, making his way in your direction. You possibly now fear for your safety and are reaching for the first available item with which to use as an equaliser if the situation develops into violence. Now just supposing that the thug is no thug at all and he is actually on his way over to apologise because he thinks he was in the wrong, or just wants to see if you are OK! But as you see him jump out of the car you react by jumping out swinging your weapon. He in turn reacts to this as he sees fit and the whole thing escalates out of control.

This whole thing happens because you have built up in your own head as to how certain people will react with situations that can result in anger. You half expect the thug to kick off and the priest to be forgiving. The fact is that both of them would have at least momentarily have been angered by your dangerous driving but they are both likely to defuse their anger in a different ways because it is expected to be like this by themselves and by you.

Situations like this can be defused by you on the simple anger level before it steps up a peg to a serious or even life threatening level. Try emulating the priest yourself next time you get cut up in your car and try apologising for your mistake, if any. It can be such a relief for some people when others actually give them a day off from being a tough guy for the day. They know that they are expected to be the tough guy at most times to most people so it is a real treat for them when somebody voluntary gets out of their car and apologises rather than an onslaught of angry abuse. Even thugs need a break!

Some people are really shocked when you are nice and non aggressive towards them, regardless of who's fault it is.

Don't however misunderstand my message. I am not trying to portray that you turn the other cheek and accept abuse from someone as a passive forgiving victim because I don't subscribe to all that bollocks! I'm just suggesting that you try to defuse a situation which is really unnecessary from going a stage further up the anger ladder..

I do apologise here if I have stereotyped any priests or thugs as being harder or softer than they would like to be portrayed, but I am neither a priest nor thug so I had to base my description on the ones that I actually know.

Another thing that comes to mind here is how aggressive we become at things that only 'nearly' happen.

Do you recognise any of these?

'You nearly killed me!'

'You nearly hit my car!'

Have you ever stopped to think about this outlook on life's possible accidents?

Have you ever thought about trying this alternative outlook and approach to the same threats?

'Thank you for <u>not</u> killing me, I'm so glad nobody got hurt'

'Thank you for not hitting my car, I love this motor'

Regardless of what or whom it is that you believe in, the fact is that your car or life has been spared to live another day. This is something to be grateful about and not angry about.

Believe me! If circumstances were a little different and someone had the balance of whether you live or die within their grasp; you will be literally begging them for the chance to live. Anger will not even come into your head – trust me I've seen it!

It's very easy to throw anger and abuse out of the car window whilst you speed away psychologically protected by the shell of your vehicle, but most of us would not act the same way whilst walking down the street if someone walked in front of us cutting us up. Most of us would just step aside and carry on regardless.

Have a real good think about all of this and how the priest and the thug are expected to act in all confrontational situations, not just road rage, and think about how different things could be if the anger was taken away from both of them.

You could then be like the priest or the thug and still be able to defuse confrontational situations in your own life without having to think that you have to act angry because it's expected of you. Think about this and try to react differently towards anger from others towards you and how freely you have been offering out anger yourself. What you can't be today, you can be tomorrow. You may even see me trading in my steel toe-cap boots for a Dog Collar, anything is possible!

You Want it Done by When?

This is the classic one liner that is commonly seen as a sketch of one-person using this phrase whilst holding their stomach in fits of laughter.

Well as funny as it seems, we are often given a task to do which is impractical, impossible or unreasonable. Yet people still get angry when we are unable to complete it!

This can also happen the other way round when we ourselves are expecting others to do something that we are not evaluating realistically. Sometimes people are setting up situations to fail before they even begin. Miracles we can do straight away but the impossible takes a little longer!

This really sums up many of the situations that we are expected to do where we and others just end up angry when it fails even though it's pretty predictable that it's doomed right from the offset.

Most of the time when you are given an unreasonable task to do, you can be pretty certain that they also are unable to do that same task themselves within the time slot that they are asking you to do it within. That's the way I see it anyway! Unless of course they are more experienced and you are not yet at that level.

It matters not whether you are old, young, fat, thin, male or female; at the end of the day you are only capable of what your own body is capable of doing or what it will allow you to do within a given time period. So if you have the practical ability, skills and knowledge to perform a given task, and it is humanly possible for 'you' to do, then you should be able to give it a fair crack of the whip and try to get it done!

I get tired of hearing people angrily moaning that they are doing the job of three people and that they do not know how they are expected to do it all. It makes them very angry! Well I hate to be a killjoy or spoil their angry moaning but one person can only do the amount of work that is physically possible by one person. Lets forget how many ways a particular set of tasks have been divided prior to this.

You as one person have managed to do as many of these tasks on your own within your current physical capabilities, so you are really only doing one person's work. It's all a matter of how you look at things.

If I asked you to drive two different cars to two different places at the same time, that comes into the category of being impossible because that physically needs two people to do that. However if I ask you to drive my children to school and also drop of my neighbour's children at their school, technically you could say that this is the work of two people, but the reality of this is that one person is quite capable of doing this task. They will not be able to both be dropped off at the same time at two different locations, but it is possible for them to both be dropped off. So although it may seem as though you are doing the job of two people, in reality it had been done by only one person so it must be one person's job. It's quite simple when you think about it or look at it from a different perspective but being able to get the brain to accept it is a different matter altogether. We get it fixed in our own heads as to how much we will allow ourselves to do for whatever the reward will be. This could be money, goods, time out, pleasure, and so on but it will be profit of some kind.

If you are stuck in a job where the workload is too demanding then look for another job if you are not able to find a way or create a change that will lighten the load for you. Never loose sight though that there will always be someone out there that will be prepared to take on your job the moment you leave because they may have a job that is even worse than yours. So in turn why don't you step up into someone else's pond who is not happy with their job. I know its not as easy as it sounds by using this outlook, it is possible. Don't chase the position of happy people because they are there for the duration or at least a long time. Chase the jobs of unhappy people if they are in a better position than you, rather than being angry.

Anger at Child Abuse

Although I have spoken on the matter of young people being physically harmed by adults within this book, here I want to touch on an area that causes anger in all right minded people. That of child abuse!

This can come in many different formats such as verbal, physical or sexual, but the area that I want to focus on here is that of sexual abuse.

It is absolutely impossible for me to even attempt to give you an exact or estimated figure of how much sexual abuse goes on against children but what I do know is that it happens!

It happened within my own family towards my sister when she was around eight years old by my biological father, and I have also spoken to literally hundreds of young girls within my teaching of female self protection to know that it goes on more than we could ever conceive. This doesn't exclude young boys either. The matter of child abuse is definitely one that has changed the whole course of my life and my outlook on the world and its hidden horrors.

When I worked as an adviser for the citizen advice bureaux; part of my training I was told that I will be hearing and dealing with problems from all types of people and some of this will be of a nature that I may find very hard to accept, with me being a right minded person. Well they were certainly right there.

I could deal with young people telling me that they were being abused by others and I was glad to be able to offer them a range of informed choices on how they can deal and tackle their problems or any abuse that they were suffering from. They were then in the position of being able to deal with matters as they see fit. Adults however are a different kettle of fish when it is they that are the perpetrators rather than being the victim. I don't want to be listening to any adult telling me that they are abusing their own child or that of another and believe me, they can come to you as a citizen advice advisor and tell you this and you can do nothing about it because you have signed a contract of confidentiality. I came to realise that I was not able to solve the ugliness of child abuse from the adult end.

It was just making me angrier more and more each time I had to listen to these sickening disclosures so I decided that I would be better off dealing with the problem from the other end, that being the young person who was the victim. I wanted youngsters and adults to become more aware of the threat of sexual abuse so that they are in a more aware position that would enable them to avoid it or at least recognise it when it does happen. Not everybody recognises when they are being groomed. This is not a book on abuse of young people but this is an area that I know has angered many people throughout the country enough for them to demand that paedophiles living near to them are made known to the public. As a parent myself I know that I and every other parent that I know of would make a statement or comment to the effect of *'I will kill anyone that touches my child.'*

However the reality is that many abusers are eventually found out and exposed and do not get killed! The problem here is that us right minded people have personal inhibitors inside of us that stop us from doing many things that we perceive as being wrong and murder is just one of them. This results in us becoming very angry, bitter and we suffer because we have heard of or know of a child that has been abused and we have not done anything about it! This is quite natural but as I've said before, you must find alternative ways to deal with your anger.

My own personal way when dealing with this particular subject is to write about it so as to educate young people or the horrors of abuse that can happen to them, but your way may be different? I would not even begin to try and tell a young person or the parent of an abused child that they should turn the other cheek and forgive the abuser because I do not subscribe to all that forgiveness bollocks! I suggest that you pursue the legal channel to deal with crimes of this nature and then find a way to deal with your anger because you cannot change your past, you can only change the future, which begins right now!

However what you must not do if you become aware of a situation of a young person being abused, is take the route of ignoring it and hoping that someone else will deal with it.

If everyone was to do this, nothing would ever get reported and abuse will always go on undetected.

If you are not sure of how to deal with incidents of this nature, here is some information that may help you.

You can phone the police on 999 and ask to speak to the child protection unit. They are specially trained and have selected officers who know how to deal with child abuse. Their main concern is for the welfare of the child and they will look into a situation to determine if they feel an offence has been committed. They will attempt to identify the person or people responsible and will try to secure the best possible evidence so that criminal proceedings can be considered.

They will have to consider whether or not it is in the interest of the young person concerned, to take legal proceedings. Whether or not there is substantial evidence to prosecute and whether it is in the public's interest that proceedings should be instigated against a particular offender. A pretty shit world eh!

Even when all of these conditions have been satisfied; the accused will still not have to prove their innocence. It will be down to the evidence collected by the police and the crown prosecution service to prove that an offence has been committed beyond reasonable doubt!

It is no wonder with all the legal hoops that we have to jump through to deal with an abuser that many abusers remain undetected and unprosecuted!

If you know of any child being abused or suspect that they are being abused then please go through the procedures described above so as to save them from further harm. If you just remain angry and suffer in silence then so does the child.

It is also worth noting here that the police have emergency power to detain a child or young person in a place of protection or prevent their removal without prior application to a court. They can also apply for a search warrant to find any child that is at risk and may need to be examined and if they think that the child's life or limbs are at risk they can do so without a warrant.

So don't just get angry - Get even but do it legally!

Anger Bullies!

I think that many people will be able to put their hands up and replace the sentence *'I am angry'* with *'I am a bully!'*

I justify this by saying that the largest group of angry people that I have seen are parents, who are being bullies towards their children and towards their partners. If you take time out to take a closer look at these scenarios you will see what I am talking about!

So often you see parents screaming heavily at children and even hitting them because they are angry with them, however the only reason that they do this is because the children allow them to, because they do not really have a choice! Also because the adults are bullies.

These self same people would not go out and scream or hit other adults that anger them to the same degree. Reason being is that the adult can return the anger and can hit back, but children generally are not able to. Children are afraid of the consequences so accept the anger and any physical abuse because they become accustomed to do so. This sadly becomes learnt behaviour and there is no reason why that battered child does not grow up doing the same thing to their children and partners through believing that this behaviour is acceptable. I think that my approach is pretty different to many others because I do not believe in hitting children! That would just make me a bully because our learnt behaviour rules tell us that we can hit children but they cannot hit us back; seems a little unfair to me and sounds like rules set up by a bully?

One day I witnessed a full-grown adult belting a child in a supermarket because the child knocked over a drink? I approached him and asked would he have hit me in the same way had I knocked over the drink? He said that he would 'not' because I looked like I would tear his head off! (As if I would be so passive). I then told him that he was a bully because he has just shown that he is hitting someone because he knows that he can get away with it, and that the youngster will not, or cannot hit him back. The guy was speechless and grabbed his child and gave a big hug and apologised.

If you are a parent or look after children in some way and I have now made you realise that you get angry or are a bully in some way to children or a partner, please stop as from now. It's not too late to change the way you are. Put the error of your ways behind you. The next time you get angry with a child for laughing too loud, spilling a drink or whatever? Ask yourself if you can deal with your anger in a different way, even if it's only finding the youngster something else to do to distract or occupy their mind for a while just long enough for you to calm down. Obviously spilt drinks happen and cannot be prevented from happening if it's a genuine accident so don't let silly things like that wind you up. It is normally only suppressed anger that manages to reveal itself when trivial matters trigger it off such as a child doing something wrong or an accident happening.

If you ever get to the stage where you want to physically hit or strike a young person for any reason at all, just stop yourself for a moment and ask yourself. *'Would I hit Jamie O'Keefe for doing the same thing? Would I hit Roy Shaw for doing the same thing? Would I hit anybody that is likely to be hard enough to put me on my back?'*

Well I can tell you now that in almost all cases the answer would be No! And the same reply would be for most other adults and the reason being is that generally; adults are less likely to tolerate bullying and the bully also realises that another adult will recognise an act of bullying and will be in a position to deal with it, whereas a young person may not.

I've discussed anger towards children but another important area to talk about is anger towards our partners!

This can lead to violence and beatings and once again I think that we will discover a bully in operation.

Here's the scenario; the husband or boyfriend comes home from a shit day at work and brings home with them a bucket load of suppressed anger. He steps into the home and sees the kids running about all over the place, the washing up not done, or whatever pathetic gripe he has that day and is going to use as an excuse to unleash his anger. It goes unnoticed that his partner has probably done the dishes three times already that day and the children have kept her busy all day, he will still only see what he wants to see and aims his suppressed anger at the person that he is supposed to love? The only reason all this is happening is because he knows that he can get away with it - he is an anger bully!

I am one of the most passive individuals that you can ever meet despite my outward appearance, yet I know that I am also guilty in the past if being an anger bully just because I knew that I could get away with it. Never the physical stuff though, I have never hit my children and the nearest I have ever come to physical violence with a partner is when one of them has physically punched, kicked and even tried to run me over, but then all I did was to stop them.

Physical violence within relationships or against children is a big 'No No' for me and I have two ex wives and four children who will testify to this fact.

I, like millions of others, did not have a book like this to help me understand and come to terms with the fact that at times, I was an anger bully. Nobody was able to advise me of the error of my ways so I had to learn the hard way!

I think that losing two families has taught me this by now but I still had to spend over 20 years discovering this lesson the hard way.

The suppressed anger that I accommodated for many years manifested itself mostly in the form of jealousy, which in turn has made me lose some special people from my life. I blame nobody but myself because I now realise the error of my ways. Hopefully the new 'anger free' Jamie has turned out to be a good catch for my current girlfriend.

Please don't make my mistakes. Have a good think about yourself and make sure that you are not blindly becoming or already are, an anger bully.

Excluding my current girlfriend, I have only ever 'truly' loved two women in my 'past' life but drove them both away from me due to my anger bullying; evolving into jealousy. Either of them could possibly have been wife number three but my behaviour prevented this happening. This is something that I will have to live with for the rest of my days but also they were both experiences that I had to go through and suffer from before I would accept and understand the sort of person I was. This has now enabled me to treat my current girlfriend like a princess. Please don't make the same mistake and lose someone that you really care for through being an 'anger bully.'

Although I am focussing here on men becoming anger bullies towards their partners and children. It is not exclusive to men. Women can be real experts in this field of being anger bullies towards their children and partners and it also happens within same sex relationships, normal friendships and also people towards their pets.

Are you an anger bully?

Ask yourself these questions:

1. Do I get angry with people who are likely to hit me?

2. Do I have a go at people because I know I can get away with it?

3. Do I get even angrier if someone tries to argue back with me?

4. Do I get angry with young people and try to show how tough I can be by acting aggressive and frightening?

5. Do you make your partner frightened to speak to you about some things because they know it will make you kick off?

6. Do you make your pet dog fear you?

Unintentional Anger Triggers

There are many occasions when your anger is switched on by somebody who may be completely unaware that they have done so and it may even be the case that their actions were even to please you in some way.

It may be by a friend who informs your work colleagues that you have just broken up with your partner so that they will treat you gently and not ask you the wrong type of questions unintentionally. Whereas you may not have wanted them to know about this aspect of your personal life because its personal to you or you feel like shit because you have been dumped or cheated on.

It may be that a surprise birthday has been put on for you but this is not the sort of thing that you are into, or that you have applied for a new job and wanted it kept secret until you had a letter of confirmation that your application had been successful but your proud parent, partner or friend has already told half the world that you are now going to have a new career. There are 1001 different reasons that a goodwill gesture or harmless or thoughtless action may cause you to become angry. Well it's time to take a chill pill and realise that although some people have angered you, it was not their intention to do so. They actually thought that they were doing something to your benefit. How can you really be angry at someone's innocent effort of doing something that they truly thought was to benefit you?

Although I write books and make my personal information available to anybody who is prepared to pay the price of my books, believe it or not, I am still a very private, shy, introvert, laid back person. I am very protective of what I let people know about me on a personal level and need to really trust someone before I open my heart to them. My reasons are that I have been shit on and mentally hurt on many occasions from the very last people that I ever expected to hurt me. People that I trusted with my life, so I now tread very carefully and do not let anybody have any information about me that could cause me to suffer. I also deal with my personal relationships in the same way and do not let anyone get too close to me because I do not want anyone to be able to hurt me. I'm not talking of physical closeness here because

I am more than capable of dealing with that; I am talking of emotional closeness because in the words of the 'Human league' *I'm only human!*

In the past when I have found out that personal information of mine has been passed around by others about me, it has made me angry. I felt betrayed by the person who has shared my information and also threatened by the new holder of this information for how they may misuse this information. It may be something silly like what my next intended career move is, or which female I am attracted to, or even where I am going to take my children on holiday, but whatever it is, it's something that I do not want shared with the world until I choose to disclose it and put it in the public domain. If I haven't shared part of my life with you personally or through one of my books, interviews or articles, then it is not public property.

I have my own reasons for keeping certain parts of my life private as most of us do.

I realised that I had a problem with anger rearing its ugly head over something as minor as this so I had to set out and do something about it. I now make it quite clear to whomever I am sharing information with, that if I am sharing something personal with them about my life then it is to go no further. They then cannot make the mistake of passing this information on without knowing that they are betraying my friendship and trust in them. I have even gone as far as telling each individual person that I trust one personal thing about me that I have not told the others. The day that the 'one thing' that each of them knows travels further than their own lips, I will know where it has come from and I will never again confide in them. I cannot confide in people that I cannot trust. My own mother and sister failed this simple test on many occasions with me so I was not even able to confide in either of them with a lot of problems that I had in life because my personal information would spread like wildfire. It did not change how I felt about both of them because I realise that they both had an addictive illness that does not always leave them in control of what they say to others. Friends are different though and if they beytrayed my trust then I would simply have to stop being friends with them. That was much easier than getting angry with them as I would have years ago. I suggest you use a similar approach with people that abuse your trust if it is intentional rather than bother with the anger route. Don't do this with those that share your information in a way that was not to cause you harm, shit happens, just make sure that you make it clear to them what's private and what's not!

There are other ways that people will unintentionally set off your anger when they really don't think that what they are doing is wrong; here's a story about a female friend of mine who was out drinking with some male friends of hers. It was all quite innocent and her husband was at home fully aware of where she was and with whom. Throughout the night alcohol got the better of one of the guys and he made a sexual advance at my female friend knowing fully well that she was happily married. She later told me about how angry she felt at what he had done knowing her current situation and the fact that they had been friends for some time now. She was shocked that he could even consider something like this. She spoke to him about it the next day when he had sobered up and he apologised. My point here though is that he did not perform like that in order to make her angry; although what he did was wrong, it was never his intention to make her angry. He obviously thought that there was a mutual attraction and that he was doing something that was going to make them both happy! Wrong move Matey!

They have resolved the matter now and the friendship will never be able to fully recover from that 'careless whisper.' However my point is that this is another example of someone being made angry when that definitely was not the intention.

Here's another example;

A few years ago I sneaked my children out of the country (legally) and took them to Florida's Disneyworld for a couple of weeks, but led their mother who they were living with, to believe that I was taking them to Barry Island in Wales. My reason for doing this was quite simple. My children did not live with me and I had recently separated from my wife and I knew that she would put a block on me taking them out of the country through her belief that I would not return with them? This was not my intention of course, which I proved when I returned to the UK after the two weeks returning the children at the time that I had arranged. Anyway my point is that I was not able to tell a single person about my intentions including my own mother and sister through fear of the in-laws finding out and this information getting into the hands of my ex wife. She certainly would have contacted the passport office and put a stop to it resulting in a cancelled holiday and the loss of thousands of pounds.

One day prior to the holiday I was out drinking with a lifelong pal who slipped up in the conversation of what a great time that I would have with my kids in Florida. I was in shock because I knew that I had not told a single person of my plans and he was also still in contact with my ex! It turned out that this 'friend' of mine had seen the holiday booking form in my house one day which explained how he knew, but the sad thing was that he could not have seen it without having looked through my paperwork whilst I was upstairs on the phone, because it was halfway down a pile of papers where I had hid it away from the prying eyes of my children! I lived alone so I knew exactly where the holiday form was. Just to confirm my suspicions of him and his prying eyes I tested him by confiding in him with something about me that was not true. A few weeks later this same information was relayed back to me quite innocently by my children who had heard it from their mother, who in turn could only have received it from my friend 'the spy.'

He abused my trust and friendship so I decided to disassociate myself from him. To this day I will never know if he did make my ex aware that I was going to take my children out of the country, or if she even believed him but it all went smoothly and I did not get arrested on my return so it was a happy ending.

So the moral of the story here is that if you are likely to become angry at someone if something about you is released within the public domain by them without your consent; don't share this information with them in the first place or make it quite clear to them that you are telling them as a trusted friend and that you do not want this trust abused!

Depressive Anger - The Hidden Killer

Have you ever considered suicide? Have you ever been that depressed that you really feel that you have nothing worth living for? Well I'm embarrassed and ashamed to say that I have been at this crossroads within my life on at least two separate occasions. It is embarrassing for me to admit to this because I am not a weak person and do not give up on things at the first hurdle, so for me to ever think like this it tells you that I have hit more than my fair share of hurdles.

I have had a pretty shit life compared to most other people that I know but a brilliant life compared to the poor, hungry and diseased families that struggle to survive in the third world and similar situations. However no matter how much better my life has been to those less fortunate than me; it still doesn't make the slightest bit of difference to me if I get hit by depression. When it comes, it comes big time and is here to stay, and one of the only viable alternatives available seems to be to get out of this world. I have not suffered from this condition for some years now and on reflection I can see that my depression was really due a lot to my anger at various situations and I just didn't know how to deal with my anger!

I was angry at the loss of my children both times when my marriages broke up, and I was angry at the whole unfair world which I didn't feel was worth being part of anymore. Luckily for me, the very thing that was taken from me, that being my children; was the very same thing that become my saviour. I 'lived' for my children, and I mean that literally and due to them I have never felt that type of anger or depression again. I even went as far as having a vasectomy some years ago to ensure that I never feel that 'life threatening anger' again through breaking up with someone and losing my children again. Alcohol was my healer through the bad times but it was also took me into the realms of danger. Although I would drink myself to sleep night after night in the early days of missing my children to take away the pain and suffering that I was going through, this drunken state also made me more vulnerable and susceptible to causing harm to myself through not having the ability to think logically or with care and consideration as to how I would hurt myself or others.

I know that many people turn to prescribed drugs or even illegal drugs to see themselves through the bad times, and much debate and discussion goes on about this subject and of how bad the drugs are for you in the long run, but my view is that if it takes away that anger that may cause you to take your own life; then it's a choice that I would not condemn until you are able to find a better alternative to ridding you from your anger and depression. My personal choice was alcohol because it was legal and I do not subscribe to the world of drug taking but at the end of the day, if you find that your anger is becoming depressive anger and may become life threatening, you should do whatever you need to do in order to save your life. Have a think about others who may be going through these type of experiences and are suffering from that hidden killer - depressive anger, because you may just be the one thing that gets them through and saves their life!

I had a close friend who suffered from depressive anger and hung himself. I was not around to be able to help him but I have also intervened and saved people taking their own lives on two other occasions just seconds from the point of no return.

On both occasions I asked what was the driving force that made them take such extreme measures and the reply on both occasions was ANGER!

Depressive Anger is a big time hidden killer!

The Child Support Agency

No book on anger would be complete without a section on this organisation. It angers both men and women for different reasons. Women because the CSA are not managing to collect payment from absent fathers where the women are of the belief that the men have thousands of pounds in disposable income that they are not using towards the upkeep of their children. Then there are the men who are without their children and have to fight for just a few hours (if any) each month to see their children and have to pay for this 'privilege' to their former partner who also claims to not have enough to live on. It's a nasty business and has turned some men to suicide due to assessments made on them by the CSA, the end result in these cases are that everybody loses.

I personally pay around £7,000 a year through the CSA, which I will be liable to continue paying for at least the next ten years. This is to an ex wife who has remarried and both her and her husband have a double declared and undeclared income as well as my contribution. So they are not exactly having it hard. On top of this they have my three children and get all the daily pleasures of seeing them every day and night before they go to bed along with the hundreds of other special moments that parents experience as part of their children growing up. These special moments are worth more than all the money that I could ever earn. I have to grasp at the few special moments that happen on the days that I have them which cost me around another £3,000 per year. I am fortunate that I live a simple lifestyle, do not smoke or do drugs, do not gamble or waste any money on myself. So I do not need that much money to live on. For the next ten years of my children growing up I will not spend money on a flash new car, house or the trimmings and furniture that come part and parcel of giving of the 'I am successful' image. That is all bollocks to me when I could spend all that money on my children making sure that they have everything that they ever need. I would rather have a threadbare carpet on my floor and know that my daughter will be able to do horse riding, than have a flash looking house and not help my children to gain all the experiences that I am able to provide for them.

The money that I pay to the CSA each week is something that I personally do not even miss! And that is the honest truth! I'm not being flash or attempting to make you believe that I have lots of money because I really haven't got a pot to piss in. I am a successful author whose hobby of writing became embarrassingly successful and began making money forcing it into becoming a business. Having my own business would allow me to create a 'nil income' for the purposes of the CSA assessment if I wanted to quite easily, but it is my choice not to do this. If I didn't want to pay, I could change my circumstances so that I do not have to pay the CSA anything and nobody could do a thing about it. But I don't! It is a choice that I have made and I am making a few sacrifices and not all financial ones, in order to do this. My frame of mind and mode of thought is that if I can genuinely afford to pay this amount each week then I will.

So now we have gotten around to our frame of mind, lets take a look at anger.

For me, anger at having to pay out all this money each year does not exist. I have no anger about this because it is a choice that I made. However I know that it is an area that makes many men mad with rage and some even get pissed off at only having to pay £20-£30 per week?

Earlier on in the book I suggested that if something is making you angry and you cannot avoid this situation, then find another way to deal with your anger if the problem is not going to go away. One alternative that you do have is to not pay the money, but that is not an option that I would suggest if you can genuinely afford to pay. Even if you believe that your wife has run off with another man, and they have taken your home and children away from you, they are still your children; your flesh and blood, your creation and probably had no part in the whole thing that caused it all to go wrong for you. Your children still need to be supported.

I can understand you not paying for your ex partner if she is on income support because she will not get your money anyway and the amount she is receiving must be enough to live on otherwise income support would have to pay more. So in this situation you can help out by buying all the other nice things that stops your child sticking out like a sore thumb as the 'poor kid' in school. When my ex was on income support I knew that indirectly through my tax and National insurance payments each week that I was providing the basic amount for the upkeep of my children. On top of this though I did all the other things that I knew that they are not going to get like the trip to Disneyworld in Florida, the quads they wanted etc..

However if your ex is not in receipt of income support and your children will benefit from your contributions and you can 'genuinely' afford to do so - put your hand in your pocket and pay up! If you can manage to buy your mates a round of drinks or go out for meals then you can afford to help out with your own children. Unless you are just a selfish bastard.

I know what it's like to queue up for free school dinners and have handed down clothes from jumble sales etc. And how I was not able to fit in with other children of my age because I was not able to discuss the same toys that they had because I never had them. Do you really want your children to go through all this and more at school and in their neighbourhood just because you are keeping the money for yourself that could make a big difference to them. For goodness sake - they are only kids once; you have the rest of your life to spoil yourself!

I do not agree with the CSA or it's way of operating but we are stuck with it so it is something that I and millions of others are going to have to put up with because we are stuck with it, so accept it!

Like I said, there are some things that we cannot change or do anything about. It is all down to how you are going to deal with your anger at this situation. Here's how I dealt with mine so that the anger did not stay with me. My anger is with the way the CSA operates. I do not have any anger towards my ex wife, her husband, or my children and have accepted that I have ten years of it left. That's nothing compared to my friend that has another 16 years of his life sentence to serve and would happily pay twice the amount that I pay just to be free.

So to make my situation as bearable as possible I have opened up a special bank account purely for this CSA payment.

Every week without fail I transfer the same amount each week from my personal account to my CSA related account which in turn is paid by direct debit each week to the CSA. I then forget about it and it all runs without any problems. Each month I get my personal statement from the bank that shows that hundreds of pounds are transferred to my secondary account to the name of J.O'Keefe and not the Child Support Agency. This doesn't change the reality of where the money is going; it just lessens the fact of me being reminded every single week that the CSA are taking my money. My anger is not sparked off again every single week. Even for those of you that are employed rather than being self-employed. If you did not pay the calculated amount direct to the CSA or your ex, they will make an attachment of earnings which you will not be able to do anything about and you will have it staring you right in the face each time you get your payslip. Result will be your weekly dose of anger with the CSA. There is no need to keep putting yourself through it if you are going to have to pay your way anyway. You may not have much of a choice as I do to create a nil income if you wanted to but try to remind yourself that you are going  to take as much control of the situation as you can. I pay because I choose too, and you should be paying for the same reason because it is your duty to as a parent. If it is not your choice then try to make the best you can of it so that you can get rid of that weekly anger.

To give a different scenario; It would be like living next door to somebody that you do not get on with and are faced with anger each time that you see them on a daily basis. If one of you move away the anger stops!

You both still exist so neither of you have changed, its just that you do not have to see each other on a daily or weekly basis so you are not constantly adding fuel to the fire.

Its not much different to the CSA payments that you have to make but if you do not have the words CSA constantly staring you in the face on your bank statement or pay slip it will definitely make you less angry and eventually you will even forget that you ever was angry. You will sometimes even forget that you pay it as you do with most direct debit payments.

I forget all about my payments now until I receive my yearly statement of account from the CSA as to how much I have paid.

Here's another way you may want to look at things. Forget about your former partner and the life she or he now has and try to focus on your children only.

Imagine for some reason that your children were taken to another country for their own safety due to war or other circumstances and possessed nothing more than the clothes on their back and only water and porridge to live on. However you were in the position to send them say £50 - £100 per week to take them out of that environment and put them in a sheltered accommodation with decent food, heating, clothing and care. You would be able to provide them with the standard of living that they have now. I'm sure that you would not hesitate in sending the money on a regular basis or even swap your own lifestyle for theirs if you could take hardship away from them.

If you are not that type of person that would make this sort of sacrifice for your own children then I have nothing really more to say to you other than you need to get a life.

How about if your child needed a life saving operation that was going to cost you £50,000? Would you not sell your car, home and work for the rest of your life in order to pay for your child to have a life? I know that I would and even give my own life for that of any of my children, so I don't see why any other parent wouldn't do the same?

My whole point is that under different circumstances, we would give absolutely anything to provide our children with at least the basic needs of food, water, warmth, shelter and security and from then onwards a better quality of life.

I know that this next statement may sound like cobblers to you but at the end of the day it's 'only money.'

You know I can remember some years ago some scumbag in the newspapers who had injected his own child with HIV infected blood so that he would not have to pay child support. Now scum like that are something that I become angry about!

For the parent out there who are chasing child support payments; you haven't really got that much to complain about in my opinion. What you don't get from the absent parent, you will get from the DSS so you don't really lose considering that you also have the kids as well!

I don't really see what you have to complain about?

I fought for seven years for custody of my first son from my first marriage, lost two homes and my business in financing it all plus my sanity. Yet I raised him for the next nine years after I won custody and never once claimed a penny in child support from his mother even though I was penniless. I lived on the breadline for most of those years to ensure that he went without nothing but it was all worth it to have my son. Money meant nothing to me compared to having my son.

So whatever your position is between you, The CSA, your ex and your children, just stop and ask yourself if your anger is really justified? Even if you feel that your anger is justified, you must still try to find a way to deal with it or if possible rid yourself of your anger!

I'm Angry Because I'm Weak

Here is something that touches us all; being angry because we are weak! Let me explain a little more.

When I was a young lad I was bullied to the extreme. I was bullied for being fat, bullied for being poor, bullied for having no visible father due to my stepfather being in prison, bullied for having an Irish surname whilst attending a British Naval Academy secondary school, and so on. But the biggest reason of all that I was being bullied was because 'I' allowed it to happen due to being weak minded and too scared to fight back.

My main problem was that I thought that if I attempted to stand up for myself, that I would get a bigger beating. This in turn made me angry with myself because I was too weak both physically and mentally to stick up for myself and would let people bully me rather than chance a bigger beating if I stuck up for myself and was unsuccessful. It was a very sad state to be in and I know that many young people have and still do suffer like this. They experience this almost every day. People will only treat you in the way that you allow them to and I sadly was allowing bullies to victimise me. I might just as well have said to the bullies *'I hereby authorise and allow you to bully me every day because I am too weak to even attempt stopping you. Please hit me as much as you want'*

I was so disgusted at myself for allowing people to treat me in this way that I was becoming angry with myself; Just as any onlooker would if they witnessed the suffering that I was going through. I became so angry because I was so weak.

Many a time you will have heard someone say *'It makes me so angry the way they treat me'* or *'I get so angry at the way they treat you.'* This is the kind of anger that I am referring to here which you need to find an alternative for. On reflection I can see that I eventually dealt with my feeling of being inadequate by embracing the concept of *'No one fears when angry.'* It was not until a gang of bullies picked on my younger sister that I was able to ignore my fear and use my anger in a positive way.

I put on my 'No one fears when angry' super hero outfit and went full steam ahead into the bullies with no thought or care for my own safety. I did not fear the consequences of my actions. I was too angry to worry about that. Someone that I cared for who was even weaker than me was being taunted, shoved, and hurt which brought on in me an explosive supercharged anger that I put to good use. The results of my actions were that even the biggest bully did not want to fight me. I still got hurt in the  process, but shit happens. I had used the anger that I had at myself and I no longer felt weak and intimidated. I was no longer going to let people bully me and from that day on they never did. The downside to this was that I was challenged to fight reguarly after that by others that wanted to gain a reputation and resulted in me having hundreds of fights by the time I left school. When I say hundreds, this is meant literally and is not a figure of speech. I tell you one thing, I never became angry at myself again for being weak because when it came to physical conflicts, I had lost my mental weakness.

This has also helped me to combat weakness in other areas of my life through to adulthood. All those years ago it took the 'no one fears when angry' concept to help me help myself, by protecting another. Had I not had my sister to protect then I may still be a victim of bullying for all I know as many adults still are. I know of many people who are bullied mentally by their partners because they are being allowed to get away with it. Some even allow it to go to the extremes of physical or sexual abuse. These victims suffer in silence and become very angry with themselves for being so weak and allowing it to happen.

If you are angry with yourself for being weak, do something about it now and rid yourself of this feeling. Do you want to feel unhappy and angry with yourself for the foreseeable future? I can tell you now that the answer is no!

You may not be able to experience the *'no one fears when angry'* feeling in the same way that I did but you may be able to find another way to deal with your anger at being weak. You must rid yourself of any person or persons from making you feel angry in this way but you must do it lawfully, but what you mustn't do is put up with the shit anymore!

It may be that you have to change your job, change where you live, change where you shop, change where you socialise, or change where you train or study; just get that person out of your face and out of your life if they are making you feel miserable and weak. Break away from the people that have nothing better to do than make you unhappy.

There are so many reasons that and ways that somebody may make you angry at yourself for being weak that I cannot give you just one method to deal with them all. But if you really want to deal with this sickening feeling then work out a way to put a stop to it today!

Always remember that *'People will only treat you in the way that you allow them to!'* and if you go back for some more they will do it to you again.

Are You Taking the Piss?

Sarcasm is used a lot by people who want to embarrass, shock or degrade another for reasons of spite, humour, selfishness, bitterness, and so on. The bottom line here is that sarcasm is very likely to piss people off and make them angry if on the receiving end; Especially if it is for the purpose of sarcasm being used for another person to get a cheap laugh at another's expense.

I consider myself to be an expert in sarcasm. I am very good at observing how people act and behave and can easily suss out what a person has a complex about within themselves. People watching is something I am very good at.

When I was young I used this ability to piss people off and make them angry. It was a game for me and I was more than ready to deal with the consequences of my actions. Now twenty years later I have fine-tuned this ability that I have and use it wisely. In my guise of self-protection instructor my role is to teach my students to become proficient in the physical application of the fighting arts and all related body mechanics that are required to deal with physical conflict. This in itself is no big deal because so do thousands of other instructors from a variety of fighting arts. Where I differ and become unique is the way that I desensitise my students to the old *'sticks and stones may break my bones but names will never hurt me'* philosophy. Also as part and parcel of your training with me, I will let you know every single imperfection that you have, be it bad attitude or bad breath! Over a period of time training with me for about six months to a year, I will take the piss out of you with sarcasm to such a level that you will never again in your life let it bother you if somebody says you are fat, bald, short etc. You will have heard it all before from me and my other fellow instructors. If anything, you will even add fuel to the fire by putting yourself on offer and pre-empting any sarcasm or 'put you downs' that they could possibly come out with. You will then have a head start and will be able to laugh off any comments that would have otherwise normally have left you angry. If I give someone a sarcastic comment to use then I may feed them for the day, but if I teach them the art of sarcasm and how it works both ways, I feed them for life! I don't really like to think that I am teaching people how to be sarcastic; I prefer to look at it that I am teaching them to deal with sarcasm so that it rids them of anger and replaces it with laughter. There is a quote that says that for every minute of anger that you have, you lose sixty seconds of happiness'!

I teach people how to handle the nasty comments that come their way so that they don't have to use their fists through anger.

I will use myself now to enlarge a little on sarcasm. Within the first few minutes of meeting me you will realise that I am overweight, balding, and have a goatee type beard and tash, but what you may not yet have noticed is that I am an OK sort of guy. So I'm fat, bald and in need of a shave, but I am also a real nice guy, even if I say so myself. But if you want to take the piss out of me, just incase you haven't noticed, I sniff a lot due to my busted nose, I have battle lumps on my forehead, a flat nose, small hands, ears and penis and different colour eyes but apart from that *'What could you not possibly like about me'?*

I have now taken away all the verbal ammunition that you could use on me to be sarcastic towards me. You cannot tell me anything that I have not pre-empted you with and told you about myself. You cannot catch me out and get a cheap laugh. You cannot make me angry by using any single factor of how I look. So lets now take a good look at you!

Have you got a complex about a certain part of your body that would make you angry if someone took the piss out of it? Well guess what? If we have ever met I have already spotted it along with all the other things that you don't think that I've spotted, along with all the other imperfections that you yourself didn't even know that you had. This is my game - do you still want to play?

This now should give you an idea as to how I train my own people so that they get rid of any complex about themselves that they may have and become fully trained experts in spotting sarcasm coming at them a mile off. They are then capable of preventing or reacting to it however they see fit according to the occasion.

Anger is a secondary reaction, which sometimes happens when somebody has humiliated or belittled you in some way. So why not learn and teach yourself to pre-empt this in some way; for instance by throwing out the punchline before they even get a chance to crack the joke. For instance if you were bald and were meeting someone for the first time who looked as though they are likely to be sarcastic at your expense you could try something like

'hi my name is ? and my head serves as a solar panel to charge me up in the sunlight'

Which may just pre-empt their *'hey look guys, egg head has arrived.'* It is the difference between you getting the laugh at no one's expense without you becoming angry, compared to them making a sarcastic comment to get a cheap laugh at your expense, with you hiding anger behind a false smile.

I personally encourage people to take the piss out of me and never feel any anger at these harmless type of comments. If I ever find that someone is being purposely nasty at me then I am capable of dealing with that in a variety of ways, but none of them are fuelled by anger.

Another way of dealing with the nasty sarcasm is to act like you don't understand. *'I'm sorry! but I don't understand what you said, can you repeat it?'*

This time everyone else is now looking at them as they try to capture the moment that existed and 'may' have caused a laugh - but is now gone! They are now more likely to embarrass themselves if they try to be funny!

There is a way to do everybody - you just have to find the way!

Anger Makes You Stronger

There is no doubt about it that angry people seem to find a reserve of strength that they are not normally aware of or put to use. Also because they become so angry they do not realise themselves as to how dangerous they can actually become themselves due to this extra boost of strength that anger has given them. This is one of the things that really sickens me when I see adults smacking children, especially when it's done with anger. They even manage to time their spoken words with the landing of each physical strike I.e. *Don't (smack) you (smack) ever (smack) do (smack) that (smack) ever (smack) again (smack)* If the child is not yet crying, they lay into them with round two.

I am totally against the striking of children. I personally don't care for any justification that you can try giving me for doing it. I have already covered this topic elsewhere in the book so I will skip the 'leave the children alone' lesson. What I want to cover here is how much forceful the strike will be to that child if it is done when angry because of anger making you stronger. If it only takes eight and a half pounds of applied force to break any adult bone in the body and only two pounds of applied force to kill somebody; what the hell are people doing in striking children whilst the adult is in an angry rage backed up by 8-28 stone in weight behind it. Babies have been shaken to death, thrown against walls and floors, and have been belted so severely that some have ended up crippled, severely brain damaged or dead. For those parents that complain of political correctness going mad because they cannot smack their own children by law, I would like to see them get in a wrestling or boxing ring with someone four times their size and strength who is angry, and see how they feel about being belted about. I really hate parental bullies!

If you are the type of person that does lash out when you become angry; please just stop yourself for a moment and make yourself aware of how dangerous you are being towards others. Remember what I said, *'It only takes eight and a half pounds of applied pressure to break a bone.'* I know, I've had to do it on a few occasions for my own survival to stop a weapon or physical attack on me from continuing. For a few moments of anger you may cause another person damage that is irreversible and you will have to live with that or it's consequences for the rest of your life. So if it is the case that anger makes you stronger and that you are more likely to cause physical damage to another person, it's time now to take on board the advice that I have given in this book and find an alternative to your anger. Another thing to think of here is of why it is also so important to defuse a situation where somebody is getting, or is in an angry rage with you.

I can remember once having an argument with a former girlfriend and really pissing her off about something which I cannot even remember now; when suddenly in an anger and rage she launched a forceful punch to my face before speeding off in her car. For me on the receiving end, the blow felt like one of the forceful blows that I would get from one of the lads in light sparring. If the blow was landed on the right spot with the force she had used, it was quite capable of knocking me out. But as it was it was misplaced and was just a blow that did not cause any effect. My point here is that this blow was something that she was not normally capable of. When I discussed the incident with her later on she had not realise the force that was actually behind the blow, she just felt that it was a light tap and nothing more, which was brought on by anger. She did not realise how much more forceful the blow had become when fuelled by anger. From that day on I made a conscious decision to not teach her any of the deadly or lethal techniques from my training system for two reasons; one being that I did not want to end up blinded or with a broken neck the next time she kicked off in an angry rage, and also I did not want her anger to turn into a serious physical assault on somebody at her work place because of a simple angry situation like this and ending with her in prison. I think my decision was the right choice because some months later she lost her temper again and physically assaulted me, tried to run me over with my own car, and smashed her way through my street door with nothing more than her bare hands. All fuelled by anger, Wow! Can I wind people up or what! Wherever that young lady is now I wish her all the best because we learnt a lot from each other on anger.

In my book 'Dogs don't know kung fu' I talk a lot about domestic violence with my main piece of advice being to avoid confrontation when someone is angry. Many a frightened child or female has realised that danger has arrived when the male clenches his fists and bangs, grabs or shows them off in a frightening forceful manner.

It is at times like this when the most serious damage is more likely to occur through being fuelled and multiplied by anger. I advise anybody in this type of relationship to get out because violent partners rarely change. So if you are not prepared to, or are not able for some reason to get out of the relationship then you are going to have to calm the big bad wolf down as best as possible. It really goes against the grain for me to advise someone to pacify an angry partner just so that the daily beating is lessened, but if people are intent in staying in this type of relationship then its all I can do. Please never forget that people can become much stronger than you are prepared for when they are angry so you may not be as prepared as you think you are.

Anger of Children

Comedian and scriptwriter Harry Enfield was pretty spot on when he created the young teenage character Kevin who was one angry teenager. However what you are seeing in this portrayal is a spoilt brat rather than an angry youngster. It's the spoilt emotions that make him funny rather than if he was just an angry lad. Much of the real true anger that children have is due to the false beliefs that they harbour about themselves or others. They may feel that they are being talked about, made fun of, or they may just feel inferior or inadequate in some way. Some of their beliefs may even be true. Nothing angers a young person more than when somebody hits on one of their 'hot spots' with comments like *'Oy fatty, spotty, ginger, lanky'*, and so on. Even when we reach adulthood we still have a complex about some things about ourselves. The difference for young people though is that they do not have the choices and ways of dealing with matters such as this, that leaves them feeling shit, as we adults do. We basically as adults are answerable to nobody apart from the law of the land when somebody makes us angry; but the youngsters are answerable to a variety of adults, be it us, teachers, guardians, other children's parents or whoever. With all these people scrutinizing them and getting ready to preach to them about how they should think and act it is no wonder they become angry when they are not able to express themselves in ways that an adult could.

So what we need to be asking ourselves is *'Why are children becoming angry?'* They do not have to worry about being the breadwinner or feeding hungry mouths, paying the mortgage or utility bills, yet they still get angry!

Most of the reasons that young people who I have seen express anger within the circles of my extended family, friends and acquaintances are two fold. One is that it is learnt behaviour that they have picked up within an adult environment where arguments involving anger were a pastime. The other reason that I have observed as to why some other groups of young people are angry a lot is because it gets them exactly what they want. There is a saying that goes *'the squeaky wheel gets the most oil'* and I seriously believe and have seen many a parent or guardian giving in to a young person's anger because it was easier than having and dealing with a confrontation. It's a case of the old *'Anything just to keep them quiet.'*

The main thing that comes to mind here is that when an adult reacts to a young person's anger, they themselves are responding automatically to learnt behaviour themselves. They have seen an angry young person before and know that it is likely to lead to confrontation if they are challenged so from past experience and learned response they have learnt that the easiest option for them is to give in to that child's demands. So in effect they are teaching that child that they can always get their own way by being angry.

So how about trying a different approach and trying an alternative route to just giving in to an angry demanding youngster.

I have already written elsewhere in the book about how adults can use alternatives themselves to deal with their own anger habits and actions, for example writing on a 'post it note' smash plate, and pin it to the wall rather than actually smashing a plate. This may be too much to expect from a young person to play along with so try and find something else that works!

How about buying them an anger hat? A big top hat or a bowler hat with which you can paint on the front *'I'm angry'* in great big letters. The young person could at least then have the option to put on this hat rather than smashing up the house, smashing toys or smashing up you. If they are the type of child that swears in anger then you could even write on the hat *'I'm fucking angry!'* It may be an idea to buy a punch bag that they can hit to release their anger. It's not a method that I would personally use because you are then connecting and associating aggressive punching with the emotion of being angry and encouraging the young person to hit out when they become angry.

However I would also say that if this method stops them from hitting you or another child then go for it until you can find something better!

Once you have found a way of diverting the young person's anger, which is calmer and more acceptable to how they have previously been, let them use it for a while until they become comfortable with it and then try to gradually work on another alternative that is a stage further away from the original display of anger.

If you also take a young person out of and away from an environment within which they are normally angry and put them into a new environment where their learnt behaviour is not known; they are very unlikely to act in the same aggressive way. For example my sister's children shout aggressively at her all the time and literally walk all over her, knowing that she will give in to their demands rather than go through conflict and confrontation with them each time, yet when they are with me or were looked after by my mother, they were as good as gold. Different people, different rules, different environment where they have to apply a different learnt behaviour because angry demands will be challenged and dealt with rather than being accepted and given in to.

Lets now take a look at some alternative approaches for you to use so that you can let a young person realize that you understand that they are angry about something?

It may even require you to change; after all if you are expecting them to change then you may have to look at how you have dealt with anger in the past.

Have you ever used any of these lines to a child?

1. *I'm fucking getting sick of this!*

2. *Don't expect any sympathy from me!*

3. *You horrible little bastard!*

4. *What you angry about this time?*

5. *I'm getting a little bored with your behaviour!*

6. *Come here and I will give you something to moan about!*

All these type of replies are aggressive verbal responses bordering along the lines of actually being threats themselves.

How about this alternative approach?

"I see you are wearing the anger hat again, why don't you tell me about how you are feeling?"

Or if it a situation where you know why they are being angry you could try this approach!

'I can see that you are angry about this so what do you think could have been different to stop you from becoming angry and feeling like this in the first place?'

The important thing here is to not be or appear angry yourself and to try to not directly agree or disagree with their feelings or actions. If you try to disagree with their anger then you just give even more grounds for them to be angry and for a longer period and if you agree with their anger then you are re enforcing that it is right for them to  be angry. You must try to stay neutral if you are going to help them with their anger management. You will still agree or disagree but will just keep it to yourself if you are going to be able to help them in a positive way.

One approach I use a lot is

'When I was a youngster a similar thing happened to me which made me feel angry; I dealt with it by? Which then allowed me to never get angry again when a similar thing happened because I was prepared for it'

There is really no point in talking to young people about anger triggers until they are of a level of understanding that they can absorb and make sense of this information. This is best left for the adults although I must say that many adults act even more immature when dealing with anger than some young people do. Reason being that adults are basically not answerable to anybody as young people are.

I Really Don't Deserve This!

How often have you heard or said the phrase *'I really don't deserve this?'*

It is done mostly at times when you feel that an injustice has been done to you and this has left you feeling angry. Well ok! Perhaps you didn't deserve the ticking off that you got from your boss for something that was not your fault, or perhaps you didn't deserve to get cheated on by your partner or lose your home or your children and the life that you was accustomed to but 'Shit happens' and you cannot undo the past or change something that has already happened. Once a moment has passed it has gone forever and remains only as a memory be it in you mind, recorded evidence such as photos or in the things that you now have to do because it has caused you to change your lifestyle in some way. It has been, left it's mark and has gone so you have no choice but to pick yourself back up, dust yourself down and get on with the rest of your life and prepare for the things that haven't happened yet. Make the best of whatever you have left and do not let anger get a grip on you because it will always strike hardest when you are at your lowest point and are too weak to fight back. Anger is just like a vulture, which preys on the weak and waits for you to die. Anger is experienced and knows exactly when to gobble you up. If you wallow in self pity and wither away into an empty shell then you will be giving someone, somewhere great pleasure and happiness with them content that they are messing up both your head and your life. You are not going to let this happen or let then take control of how you feel for the rest of your life. You are going to give yourself a kick up the backside and snap out of this mode of feeling sorry for yourself and this helplessness.

So maybe you don't deserve what has happened to you but that moment has gone. It will take time to get over it depending on what has happened to you and that may be minutes, hours, days, months or years because *'Time takes time'* and it will be different for everyone depending on the circumstances.

So if you cannot change the past then concentrate on changing the future.

There is no point in sitting idly back and doing nothing because the result you will get from doing nothing is nothing!

When my first marriage ended my world ended because my only child was taken away from me. I went through years of depressive anger and could have easily have taken my own life due to the state that my mind was in. I had nobody to turn to for support and comfort in my hardest moments apart from my two alcoholic parents and a drug-addicted sister who were all wrapped up in their own lives with their own problems. All I really had in my whole life was my son who I was besotted with and he had now been taken away and given a new man to call daddy. Absolutely everything that could have gone wrong for me at that moment in my life did. I practically invented the concept of *'Feeling sorry for myself'* along with its attached phrase *'I don't deserve this!.'*

I could have rotted away within my own self-pity due to the loss of my family, home, business and with also turning to alcohol as my companion it did nothing to help my logical thinking.

It is this awful depressed stage of my life that always flashes back at me when I see a homeless person out on the streets, knowing that I was only a small step away from joining them myself and all due to one single drama in my life. I always wonder to myself of how they have suffered or what course of events has forced or made them choose this lifestyle. I didn't deserve what had happened to me but I couldn't change it so I decided to do something about it. After all I couldn't lose because I was starting off with nothing! I went from being homeless and destitute owning nothing more than the clothes on my back and then fought for seven long years to get custody of my son. I lost my fight time and time again because I had nothing and the courts were at that time very bias towards the mothers having custody. But in true style of *'if at first you don't succeed - try try again'* I did, and eventually won.

I then raised my son, got a house, a life, a business and picked up my new life all because I was not prepared to give up and die at the first hurdle which made me say *'I don't deserve this!'*

The anger still stayed with me for many years but eventually disappeared. I will never forget what my first wife did to me but I am now able to live with it without anger as I have also done with my second divorce, which ended in similar circumstances.

I am not going to tell you that life is wonderful and a bed of roses because I personally think life is pretty shit. However if you can work at getting rid of your anger then you can at least have a better quality of life than you would have with an angry life. If I was to reflect back on my life I could attribute my current success with all being due to my not giving up at that first hurdle when I felt that I didn't deserve what had happened to me. but nah! I put my success down to my good looks and my Mr. Universe physique.

So pick yourself up my friend from whatever it is that has knocked you down and stop feeling sorry for yourself because you will only drive people away from you. Not many people can tolerate for too long, those that moan and feel sorry for themselves. Patience and empathy do both have a shelf life and a burn out rate, so do not over use these qualities with those that do listen to you because eventually you will begin to piss people off rather than have them want to support you. Don't use that tried and worn out phrase *'well if they were true friends they would understand'* because if you were also a true friend then you would not put your proverbial shit on their shoes because sooner or later they will find it easier to avoid you rather than having to keep cleaning their shoes. Get rid of anger and get on with your life! You deserve it so work for it!

Oh Ho! Here Comes Mr. Angry

Mr. Angry has many hats; one day he will be Mr. Jealous, the next Mr.Spiteful, and the next Mr.Hardoneby - but no matter which hat or disguise he wears you will always see quite clearly on his birth certificate the name Mr.Angry!

The problem with Mr.Angry is that he is very dissatisfied with his own life and feels that he deserves better. Why should Mr.Nice get all the nice friends or Mr. Hardworking get lots of money and a nice car and home? It should all be going to Mr.Angry according to him! But the sad thing is that if Mr.Angry stopped being angry for a moment, he would see that he could have all the things

that Mr.Nice and Mr. Hardworking have but he is just too busy being angry. Being angry is a fulltime job leaving all other things in life as part time.

I talked in the book of how you can use sarcasm to deal with your own complexes to stop others being able to use it on you, by you pre-empting them. But some people use it in a very nasty and angry way.

I once knew a guy that spent much of his time day after day knocking and slagging people off, that this became the whole purpose to his sad life. We all moan at sometime or slag someone off at times, that's life, but this guy did it from the moment he came within your company until the moment he left. There was always this great sigh of relief when he had gone. I eventually had to distance myself from him because his sarcastic and snide comments about other people were making me feel depressed. You could win the lottery and he would find something wrong with the person presenting you the cheque, picking the balls, or the shop that you bought your ticket from. He was so angry that every time he walked into a place where others and me were gathered you could guarantee that someone would say *'Oh ho here comes Mr.Angry'.*

If I said something to him like *'look at that lovely looking girl that guy has pulled over there'* he would come back with *'Yeah but you can bet she has been round the block a few times and without all that makeup on she would look like a right dog'*

Can you see the type of guy or gal that I'm talking about? I bet you already know one? They just haven't got a nice word to say about anything or anyone. I once said to my Mr.Angry

'I saw a friend of you son's at the shops today, he said he was going to pop round yours tonight to see your lad for a while' and to that Mr.Angry replied

'Yeah more like he is coming round to stuff himself with all the free crisps and sweets he can get.'

Poor old Mr.Angry can only resort to finding a bad side in everybody because he is judging the rest of the world by is own standards! He is bitter, selfish and greedy due to repressed anger that he has been carrying around as baggage and will probably never change. Even if I was to give Mr.Angry a free copy of this book in the hope that it would help to change him, he would probably say *'He's only given me this book because he can't sell them.'* That's Mr.Angry for you!

My whole point within this section of my book is to help you spot a Mr or Mrs Angry within your circle, which should be very easy.

There are some thing's that you wouldn't see even if it were staring you right in the face? Well it is time now to do just that and look in the mirror and ask yourself if you are looking at Mr. or Mrs. Angry?

Have a real hard and long think as to whether other people are seeing you as Mr or Mrs. Angry and you haven't realized it before. If so it's time to make change within yourself and do something about it now before you lose more than you realize and really have something to be angry about.

Fearful Anger

The adult dog fears for the safety of her pups when another person or animal comes near to them so automatically she returns a display of aggressive anger in an attempt to keep all oncomers at a distance. The mighty Swan will hiss and launch at you if you dare to go near to it's personal space and the snake will strike faster than you can blink an eyelid if you are within a threatening range. All these incidents and many more within our own human environment are sparked off by fear, with anger being the second emotion and reaction. This is another slant on 'no one fears when angry'.

I have discussed already of how real true uncontrollable anger can wipe out any fear that you have even if it's only for a fleeting moment. Also of how it can give you power, ability and courage in these times of need but I am now talking of how fear as the first emotion, turns into anger when there is a need to protect our loved ones; just as I did as a young lad when I feared for my sister's safety and ran angrily full ahead into the group of bully boys who were taunting her. It would be the same for a mother who was to witness her child being led away by a stranger or the lion looking after her cubs. In all these type of scenarios we never consider using sensible debate because the panic attack that comes with fear immediately turns us into a superhero with a few moments of unexplainable strength and ability. This is fearful anger created by fear. When we feel this emotion our physical capabilities just rise to the surface fully charged and ready for battle.

We are very protective over our personal space and that of the ones that we care for and become fearful if this personal space is invaded. We put a value on this invisible space around us and will fear for our safety if this space is invaded by someone that's uninvited. Our imaginary space that sits around us or our loved ones, be it big or small, is an 'invitation only' area.

It is this type of anger that arises in this sort of situation that I see as being 'good anger' which comes from fearful anger. It is a natural part of our makeup for our basic survival. It is a gift that you will be grateful for at some time in your life.

So when talking of ridding yourself of anger, fearful anger in situations like these is excluded because one day it may just aid you in your survival.

Do you ever remember seeing the classic children's movie 'Ghostbusters' where the calm looking ghost in the library suddenly turns into an angry ghost when it's space is invaded by the Ghostbusters?

This is an example of fearful anger showing itself and warning the Ghostbusters to back off and stay away. It is also important for your own safety that you do not unknowingly step into another person's personal space if it is likely to frighten them in some way. If you were to unknowingly do this and the person thought that you may not back off at their first growl, they may just go straight through and fast-track to a physical strike before you even realize what's going on within their head. They could be wrongly believing something that's not true and hearing the little voice in their head telling them that you are about to do something to them and that's why you have 'unknowingly' invaded their space. You really need to be careful around some people. A few years ago a man was stabbed through the eye on a train and died due to sitting in the murderer's personal space 'unknowingly'.

Actually - You Don't Own the World

We are all guilty of seeing the world from our own perspective, but for some people this perspective and outlook is a thing that some people are guilty of for all their lives. We seem to think that our preferred way of doing things is 'the way' and that everybody else on this planet should also do things in this way as well, and when they don't it makes them angry. We assume that the way we see things is the way that they really are or the way they should be. Well I'm sorry folks but there are millions of other people on this planet that do things differently to you. You do not own the world and you cannot dictate how others should spend their lives or how they choose to live. It may really anger you that your partner does not squeeze the toothpaste from the bottom of the tube as you do or prefers to wash up after dinner rather than as they are cooking, but so what? They have their personal preferences and you have yours as to how you like to do things, so why get angry about it? It's really no big deal!

You are creating anger within yourself simply because you have set up a defined list of rules on how you want to live your life and how you expect others to follow your rules. Who has suddenly made you the leader? How about you suddenly following their set of rules and see how that makes you feel? Either way whether you follow their rules or your own, you are going to get angry with them. Damned if you do and damned if you don't. So how about giving this a try; Just lead your life according to your rules and don't expect others to follow or abide by them in any way. This is not possible with young people that need guidance but with adults you should give this a try. If your partner wants to leave the cap off the toothpaste and this is not acceptable to you, its time to learn how to accept that they are different to you. If you each have your own tubes of toothpaste then you can both treat them as you wish. If you still find it a problem with you seeing their tube sitting on the bathroom shelf with the cap off then suggest that they use a cosmetic or travel bag to put the toothpaste tube in even if you have to buy it. For the price of a few pounds you could certainly reduce your anger. After all you are only affected by it if you can see it and most of your other problems can be dealt with in a similar manner.

If you read through the section on the Child support agency you will understand how things do not affect you so badly if they are not continuously pushed under your nose, even if they do still happen, but happen out of sight.

If you are in a relationship you will over time find dozens of little things that will make you angry about your partner and they will see the same in you. Isn't it strange how when we first fall in love that we do not bother too much about our partners habits, yet as the candle begins to fade the habits seem to hit you right in the face!

I've got habits myself that even anger me at times and I live alone so I can imagine how annoying these things can be for anyone that has ever had to stay or live with me. They can become a real big problem.

The important message here is to not try change people if they do not want to change. Just find ways to stop their annoying habits from angering you by trying to disguise or avoid them in some way. Either avoid seeing them or get used to them and try to remind yourself that you too have annoying habits and attributes that really irritate people. If you are not prepared to change 100% then don't expect other people to do so either. You don't own the world!

Two's not Company - Three's a Crowd

One thing about anger is that it almost always takes two people to instigate a situation of anger.

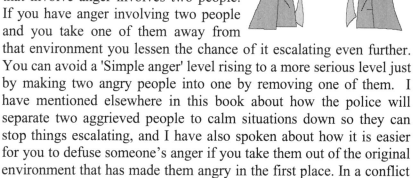

Obviously if it's the weather that you are angry about then that's nothing to do with another person unless you believe in rain dancers. So most environments that involve anger involves two people. If you have anger involving two people and you take one of them away from that environment you lessen the chance of it escalating even further. You can avoid a 'Simple anger' level rising to a more serious level just by making two angry people into one by removing one of them. I have mentioned elsewhere in this book about how the police will separate two aggrieved people to calm situations down so they can stop things escalating, and I have also spoken about how it is easier for you to defuse someone's anger if you take them out of the original environment that has made them angry in the first place. In a conflict situation where two people are kicking off with each other it is definitely not something that I would class as 'Two's company'

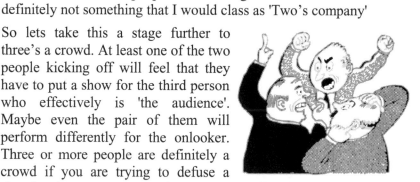

So lets take this a stage further to three's a crowd. At least one of the two people kicking off will feel that they have to put a show for the third person who effectively is 'the audience'. Maybe even the pair of them will perform differently for the onlooker. Three or more people are definitely a crowd if you are trying to defuse a situation between two people. It may even be the case that you are trying to defuse a situation where somebody is targeting you which is becoming increasingly difficult if they are acting up for the audience. It may even be you that is the one putting on the show because you do not want to lose face by backing off or talking things down in front of your audience through fear of looking weak. It may even be the third person that's the angry one who is instigating two calm people to get angry towards each other for some reason. This is a common scenario that you normally associated with troublemakers and shit stirrers.

So two's not company and three is definitely a crowd if you are trying to resolve some matters in a calm non-aggressive way. So try your hardest to get all situations down to just one person only so that you or an independent person can sort matters out easier.

Anger Actors

I had a friend some years ago that for some strange reason had to get angry every single day and displayed this within every conversation that he had with you. He wasn't really angry with most of the things that he spoke about but for some strange reason he felt that he had to display the emotion of anger when speaking to other people. His problem was that he wanted to be recognized as a tough guy, hard man and gangster; all things that he wasn't! He was very insecure within the lad culture and wanted to be respected by others for being tough rather than being laughed at for being a wimp. He used the display of anger to hide behind and to disguise how he really felt. He wanted people to think that he was not someone to be messed with but in reality people were just laughing at him and did not want him in their company. Basically he was a pain to be with and he was always an embarrassment due to the way he would always put on the anger act. He was an 'anger actor.' He would never switch off from acting the part and he truly believed that those around him actually respected him but he had nobody's respect.

His classic trademark was to say things like *'don't start me off because you know what I'm like when I'm angry'* and he would combine this with being angry at someone in an attempt to convince you that he was going round to sort somebody out. He never did go and sort anybody out because he was just an actor and later became known as someone who makes idle threats. His sad attempt at trying gain respect from people by anger acting did not work from him. All it did was make people disrespect him. We see anger actors all the time on TV; some convincing, others not, and the guy I knew definitely was not. Do you know an anger actor or are you possibly one yourself? Have a real good think about it and check that you are not trying to portray yourself in this way. At times of confrontation many people will use anger acting as a form of defence to stop the confrontation progressing to violence, which can be a good form of self protection if used convincingly. So if putting anger to good use in this type of way is going to benefit you by keeping the wolves from tearing you apart, then use it, otherwise the vultures will be there to collect what's left of you.

Contributions

I thought it would be good to interview different people on the subject of anger and just let them speak their mind on how they feel about anger and areas related to it!

Interview 1: Kevin F.

Jamie,
Good subject matter; one that I can really comment on, but not in one sentence.
Anger (Angry) can be mad, furious, enraged, irate, raging, incensed and wrathful. So in a true sense these emotions or reactions must be stronger than fear, fright, dread, horror, terror and so on, at the moment in question. Yes, in the heat of the moment someone can be furious or enraged with a certain situation that may prompt that individual to react in a certain way. A prime example would possibly be an attempted mugging, raping or an unprovoked attack. It will usually be that the person will feel fear after the incident, because of the state of mind the person was in at the time, it never allowed them to be scared. This is a prime example, but Jamie, it doesn't begin to answer your question.
I've just explained about a brief spell of anger, e.g.; you are attacked, get hurt (or not), it makes you angry then you hit back without thinking, yes you have no time to think of fear.... but it's completely sporadic.
I will be precise and explain why I believe anger cannot 'always' overcome fear. When I was in the French Foreign Legion I spoke to a person who had just returned from the Bosnian conflict, where he was serving in the tanks. He explained that one of the sergeant's jobs was to look out the hatch for snipers over a 360 degree then close the hatch. Snipers would just lay in wait and fire at random. In his case the sergeant was literally cracking under the intense pressure of having to open the hatch, he was crying tears about not seeing his family again and trembling with fear. He was getting very angry about the situation but could not control his emotions.

The person I was speaking to just remarked that they get paid extra for doing these tasks, where the normal soldiers don't.

Another real example.... Quite recently someone I knew had a dispute with a certain group of people that was escalating. The person was threatened, he didn't seem too bothered. Then they made more threats only this time he felt his immediate family was in danger. I spoke to him, and he was extremely angry, scathing. But it did not detract from his fear as he saw the threats as very serious, no matter how angry he became the element of fear was too overwhelming. He spoke of feeling ashamed as well as upset, but gave way to his fear. It was only a threat (not reality), but enough to be sufficient.

Women who learn self defence are often taught that you must get angry/aggressive with the assailant, for it is your only means of survival. The key is to train them to react instantly for if they think even for a second then they can freeze. In this case, anger can temporarily overcome fear; it must be a reaction that thinks only of survival to escape. For after the attack they will get more scared.... fear was pushed aside for that brief time. Again, this is instantaneous.

'What possessed you to do something as stupid as that'.... the calm after the storm. Yes this could be any scenario but we've all heard it. Again, it's a reaction to a situation.

Jamie, to have that anger that passionately overcomes fear totally, stems from something. For example; a question for you; what is stronger the passion of love or hate? For the saying is love conquers all is it not? Take the martyred Christians in Roman arenas, they neither hated nor feared their persecutors, so in their case love conquered fear. There are reports of them dying with smiles on their faces...... it definitely was not anger.

When a person has a rage burning inside of him; a passion called revenge that is fuelled by hate, for whatever purpose, then that can overcome fear.... I don't mean just briefly as I've mentioned earlier. When you can only think of revenge, not eating, sleeping or drinking until you achieve your goal that is not a flash in the pan anger but a cold hateful anger with one objective.... yes, that doesn't even acknowledge fear.

So love and hate both overcome fear.... but which is the strongest passion? They can both seem eternal.

Have you ever seen the star trek films, the wrath of Khan is a prime one. In these films the hatred that Kirk has for Khan and vice versa, knows no fear.... it is all about revenge and goes on and on in the different episodes.

To conquer the fears that may lurk deep inside, anger may not be appropriate. But an understanding of oneself.

On a high wire commando course, I've seen people hesitating scared to jump, even after watching other people do it.

'Get aggressive, do it', are the screams of the instructors.... they couldn't. *'You are holding the rest up, if you make us lose I'm going to make sure you....'* out of fear they've then jumped. As we were timed as a group against the clock, the repercussions prompted the jump more than the get aggressive approach. Why? Because it's an inner fear, a lack of confidence.... not a spontaneous reaction to a sudden incident.

An Infantry unit when advancing on an enemy position are taught aggression, partly because it allows you no time to think of fear. Bounding forward giving cover fire, the Charlie and Delta sections are screaming, gathering momentum as they get nearer the target. One section moves, the next is giving cover and so on. It's aggression, speed and momentum. However, if one of the sections is pinned down under heavy fire, then it's much more difficult to get moving again. Which is why it's important even suffering losses to keep the momentum going.

Maybe the answer is in the opposite. For what is the opposite of fear? Is it love? or is it anger? For as I've said anger can overcome fear. However, if the element of fear is stronger, as is often the case as people fear fear, more than the result of fear, then it triumphs over emotional anger. There is no fear in love.... that's a quote from the Bible. Vengeful hatred knows no fear. Love knows no fear.

Jamie, you've touched on a subject that I find very interesting. I hope I haven't bored you. I'll forward to reading the book soon.

Kevin. 1998

True Story

ANGER by James C - Sept 2000 Colorado Springs, USA

In retrospect anger has had a lot to do with my life. Perhaps far too much. I think maybe writing it down this way will help me as well as (hopefully) pass on life-lessons that cost me a lot.

To start I suppose a brief background is in order. My childhood was unremarkable but I will give you a brief synopses. My Mother was an English girl who yearned to explore the world so in her early twenties she left Devon, England and went to Germany, while there she lived a somewhat carefree life and basically enjoyed her independence. She met an American soldier stationed in Germany and they were married in the early 1960s. They moved to America together- where she experienced the barbaric southern region of the United States in the 1960s. Due to this experience to this day she dislikes the US intensely, perhaps understandably. Anyway, I was born in Huntsville, Alabama in 1967. Their marriage had been horrible for quite some time. It seems my biological father was a womanizer and drunkard. Only pride had kept my Mother from leaving him prior to my birth. Once I was born she decided keeping herself in a horrible situation was her business but she had no right to do the same to her just born son. So it was just Mom and me against the world for a time. Living in poverty in an Alabama mobile home court. When I was 3/4 years old she met another American soldier named Ed who, after a brief courtship, she married. Shortly after their marriage the three of us moved to Germany where my new father was assigned by the US Army. When I was 5 years of age my parents adopted a 3-year-old boy named Mustafa who was half German and half Turkish. I was selfish, jealous and resented him greatly. Our relationship never much improved either. He had almost every little problem a child could have. He was a thief, a chronic liar, a pyromaniac, and a bed-wetter who stuttered. Our perfect little family was coming together nicely. We spent the next several years primarily in Germany, which was perfect in the fact that we could fairly regularly drive through Belgium and then take the Ferry to England to visit my Mother's Family. They were an interesting bunch her family.

On the surface they were *'oh so proper'* but underneath.....well! that was something else. But more on that later. They were pleasant enough to me even though they hated my biological father. I guess they had dreamed of my Mother marrying some English blue blood who could have legitimized their fantasies of being *'upper class'*. Well so much for that. To them my natural father was *'white trash'* at best and they didn't think a great deal more of my stepfather. Regardless of how they felt, Ed was, and is, a good man. He did the best he could to provide for us. By spending so much time in Europe for my mother's sake he effectively destroyed his relationship with his own family in the United States. As for me and how I was turning out. I was an overweight little boy who was painfully shy around girls and sought acceptance from my peers through my sense of humour.

I was a fat little clown. Although I looked at sports as an excellent way to gain acceptance I was afraid to fail so I never even tried. My own love at that time was reading. I loved books. My imagination soared as I imagined being <u>loved, respected, feared and popular</u>. All the things I was <u>not</u> in life. Don't get me wrong - I had friends, and my parents loved me very much. I just didn't feel like I belonged anywhere. That was all soon to change. In the early 1980's my father's military career was coming to a close and my mother decided that regardless of what the rest of us thought we were moving to England to live. I was miserable at the prospect; although I had spent very little time in the US it had become almost a magical place in my mind. Kind of like Disneyland. A place where I would be all I had ever wanted to be and more; Going to an American school for Army dependent children I had watched my friends leave every few years to return to the US. Returning to cars, pretty girls, the prom; the American Dream. I know how ridiculous this sounds but that's what I thought awaited me in the great and wonderful United States. Here was my mother though, selfishly making us move to England. My father, brother and I were all very unhappy at the prospect but my mother was adamant.

So in 1981/1982 we moved to Reading, England. My father still had about 2 years to go in the US Army so he would remain in Germany, We moved early because my Mother wanted my brother and I enrolled in the English school system. So they bought a house on Dee Road in Tilehurst. Our street was surrounded by a council estate and wasn't that far from 'Stoneham Boys School' which is where my brother and I were to go school. I had just turned 15 and was still overweight and shy but I was also quite tall. I was very bitter and absolutely furious at my mother. In my mind I absolutely refused to adjust to my new life. I still remember how horrified I was to be fitted for a school uniform, something I'd never had to wear before. It was a culture shock. I was sullen, bitter and full of hate. My mother was all to blame, so I thought! How dare she ruin my dream of this utopian America. Almost every day that my brother and I went to school and came home again, I was literally followed all day by children who teased and ridiculed the only American they had ever actually met. It got worse because my old self-defence tactic of using humour had mysteriously disappeared. Although quite large I didn't retaliate either, which only encouraged them more. The teasing was so bad that I would eat my lunch in empty classrooms, just staring out the window wanting to attack and hurt all my tormentors. This went on day after day for weeks. My poor mother got the brunt of it because everyday when I got home, I would scream out of how much I hated England, why did she make us move here, I had no friends, etc, etc. She cried often and that is something I remember which I regret to this day. My brother was adjusting quite a bit better than I was. He was making friends and assimilating quite well. It took me a lot longer. I still remember my first friend there. His name was John Shonfield and he was a 'rocker.' His technique was also humor and his zany antics in the classroom even caused me to briefly smile. One day he came up to me in class but instead of making more jokes about Americans or tormenting me, he actually was friendly. He invited me to stop by his house after school, which I accepted. I had a friend now but I still remembered all those that had teased and tormented me for so long and I swore revenge. Shonfield and I spent a lot of time together and through him I guess I sort of 'connected' with a few others who for various reasons were outcasts of some sort.

None of us smoked, had girlfriends, played sports or did anything that would make us stick out or be popular. Had this continued I wonder what I sort of person I would be now. I will never know however, because an important event was about to happen that would change me dramatically, His name was McNabb, up to this point I had been in several fights in my life but nothing I would call brutal. Just your typical schoolyard fights. I was large for my age and was certainly capable of violence, I had just avoided it for the most part until now. So here I was now. Fifteen years old, large and part of a small group of outcasts. Then came McNabb, who would have been insignificant had it not been for the event that he caused. He too was overweight and large but he had the reputation of being a 'tough guy' plus he was a skinhead. Skinheads were something I had never encountered before and frankly their appearance and pack mentality scared me. Ironically they had never teased or tormented me at all. Then word reached me that this McNabb character was talking about me quite a bit. I was large and the last few months had showed I was docile so I guess he thought I was a safe target. One day while changing for rugby he stood there teasing me and making various derogatory comments about me and Americans in general. It was actually quite tame compared to what had already been said to me but I think it was 'the final straw' so to speak. A teacher walking in at that point prevented me reacting or retaliating right there and then. But as those morning classes passed I could think of nothing else but McNabb. I hated him with all my heart. Anger had gotten its grips on me and made me fantasize about hurting him as brutally as I possibly could. Even Shonfield's jokes and attempts to cheer me up did no good. I was consumed with fury, anger and hate. I was literally shaking with anger. I vowed at lunchtime that this matter would be solved.

Only my Friend Shonfield knew how angry I was and how much this was really bothering me. I confided to Shonfield that I planned to find McNabb at lunchtime and then fight him. As time passed leading to lunch my anger and rage that had built up over months caused the whole McNabb situation to be blown completely out of proportion within my own mind.

When lunchtime finally arrived I headed right to where I knew I would Find McNabb. Shonfield came with me, as sort of moral support I suppose. Either that or he just wanted to watch a fight. On the far side of the school was a restroom (toilet) that had long been a popular place for the smokers to gather and smoke cigarettes. The teachers knew what was going on and pretty much ignored it. One thing that honestly had not occurred to me as I walked to my confrontation with McNabb was how perfect the location was to make 'my stand' and release my anger. Most of the tough guys in school smoked so naturally they tended to gather in that restroom. What was about to happen would be witnessed by almost every skinhead, psychobilly (70s hybrid of teddyboys crossed with punk) and tough-guys (or want-to-be tough guy) that Stoneham Boys School had. By the time I reached the restroom the potential confrontations was causing me to shake uncontrollably. But as furious and full of hate as I was I didn't think to be afraid. My anger overrode any fear that I had. This fight and anger release was something that just had to happen. With Shonfield behind me I walked into the restroom, It was full but I paid no attention to anyone except McNabb who stood talking to a few other guys. At this point I must state that this was a fair fight - McNabb was the same size as me and had enjoyed the reputation as being 'hard'. His back was to me so I walked up to him and tapped him on the shoulder. When he turned and faced me he didn't appear angry or afraid, just maybe curious what the hell the 'yank' wanted. I mumbled some kind of question like *'Here or Outside?'* and before he even had a chance to respond I kicked him as hard as I possibly could in his groin. I had a lot of rage built up inside me and I think it was all offloaded in that kick. As he doubled over I grabbed his head bringing it down ramming my knee into his face and as hard as I possibly could. He immediately dropped to the floor. Shonfield told me later that the other people in the restroom started cheering me on as soon as I kicked him but I don't remember any sound. I do, however, vividly remember kicking him again and again as he lay prone on the floor. He curled into the fetal position as I kicked him in the head, face, back, anywhere I could. I learned later from witnesses it was about this time that McNabb lost consciousness, but at the time I didn't know or care. This was for every little bastard who had ever called me a name, ridiculed me or teased me in any way. This was for my mom who made me live here and this was for every girl I secretly liked who didn't even know or care that I was alive. I had a bucket load of suppressed anger that had been waiting a long time to get out. I don't remember exactly how long I kicked him but I remember when I dragged him into one of the urinals his body was limp and lifeless; he did not resist. At the stand-up urinal I dragged him to, I began smashing his head against the porcelain. All sense of reason had left me. After bashing his head against the urinal a few times several pairs of hands grabbed me and pulled me away from him. I was so excited that my whole body was shaking and I felt like I was hyperventilating. Little by little my hearing and awareness of all the people present was returning to me. Shonfield was frantically yelling at me to leave, that the teachers were coming, we had to go, we had to go! I just stood there looking down at McNabb for the moment. He wasn't moving at all and all I felt was a total satisfaction, the likes of which I had never known. The teachers arrived within a few moments and I mingled with everyone else who ran out of the bathroom. Once Shonfield and I returned to the main yard where everyone hung out at lunchtime, I tried to calm down and look as inconspicuous as possible. My hearing and vision had returned to normal but I was shaking uncontrollably and could barely speak. Although Shonfield and I stayed away from others I still noticed I was getting a lot of strange looks from the other boys. I was still too shook-up to give it much thought. We spent the lunch period trying to avoid teachers. I kept waiting far the inevitable capture (for lack of a better word) by a teacher but it didn't happen. I began to panic a little and actually began to worry that I may have actually killed McNabb and the Police were on their way.

Turns out I didn't kill McNabb after all. The teachers managed to wake him and he left school immediately for medical attention. I'm sure it came out who his assailant was but I was never questioned or confronted about the incident by teachers or police. That night at home I lay in bed playing the incident over and over again in my mind. I didn't feel guilty for doing it, just scared that I would be in all sorts of trouble. McNabb did not return to school for about two weeks so naturally the rumors flew that he had been hospitalised, with serious injuries. With each day that passed in which I wasn't arrested by the police, the better I felt. I had also begun to notice the advantage to my brutal assault of McNabb. The teasing and torment stopped immediately. To my amusement I even realized several of the boys who had so loved to ridicule me before now seemed desperate to befriend me. That would not be happening though, I remembered everything and I would not *'forgive and forget.'* I would just smile at their pathetic attempts to get on my good side and ignore them; that seemed to make them even more nervous. My friend Shonfield took a perverse delight in telling these same people how I hated them and would one day attack them as well; I am ashamed and embarrassed to say that at the time I enjoyed their fear although I really had no plans to take my revenge on them. Several of them were quite a bit smaller than I, and I've never been a bully. Then another side-effect of my new found reputation came about. I came to the attention of several of the Stoneham skinheads. The fact that I had gained this fearsome reputation by beating one of their own didn't seem to bother them; As it turned out McNabb was an infamous bully who was disliked by most - even the other skinheads.

By this time I was becoming quite knowledgeable of the various subcultures and I was absolutely fascinated. Stoneham had quite a few skinheads, smoothies (normal kids), psychobillies, a few rockabillies (70s hybrid of teddyboys and Bluegrass) and even a small handful of Mods. The skins interested me the most because at that time having a fearsome appearance was something that interested me greatly. Shortly after moving to England I had become a 'Madness' fan so I had the flattop haircut made popular by the singer 'Suggs.'
I had seen a program on BBC called '40 Minutes' that did an episode on skinheads and the punk band 'Combat 84.'Although I bad no interest in football and knew nothing of politics

something about skinheads just enthralled me. So after the McNabb incident when the local skins began being friendly to me I was certainly receptive. My Mother knew nothing of the fight but she had noticed I seemed a lot happier, so when I asked for money to buy some new clothes she did not object at all. She was probably a little curious when she saw my new 'outfit' consisting of bomber jacket and Doc Marten boots, but I doubt she was alarmed or concerned in any way. So now here I was wearing 'skinhead' clothes but with a tall flattop haircut. This served to introduce me to the psychobillies who assumed I was one of them. They even loaned me music tapes to listen to. I became a big fan of 'The Meteors' (and still am) but other than that I had no interest in the psychobilly scene. My new friends introduced me to bands like Sham 69, The Business, 4-Skins, Last Resort and of course Combat 84. When several of them tried talking me into finally getting my head shaved I must admit I couldn't put up much of a fight. So off we went to the barbers where I had my head shaved so I could look just like my newfound friends. I still maintained my friendship with the psychobillies. For some reason at that time at least: in Reading skins and psychobillios got along really well. Aside from haircuts we even looked the same. We were violent, we were intimidating, and people feared us. As this change was taking place I saw less and less of Shonfield. He just didn't fit into my new life. After all we had been through together I just casually dismissed him from my life. He had long hair and listened to heavy metal music and my new 'friends' hated him for that. One day hanging out in Prospect Park with my fellow skins a few of them saw Shonfield Balking in the distance and actually chased him. I did nothing to prevent it. Luckily he got away before they could catch him so he wasn't harmed. But to this day I am ashamed that I did not prevent them chasing him home. I am sorry John. You were a better friend to me than all those skinheads combined. I'm sorry.

So now after dumping the old group of friends in favor of the new group I found that people at school looked at me differently. Some avoided me and others tried their best to be in my good graces. One day the Headmaster walked up to me outside of school and actually publicly berated me for my 'paramilitary appearance.' I had become a ring-leader of sorts to the younger skinheads in school who all wanted to be just like me. I knew that being me wasn't all that great but I wasn't going to admit that to them. I spent more and more time hanging out at Prospect park drinking beer and even occasionally sniffing glue from a bag. I was quite the pathetic spectacle but didn't realize it then. Periodically people from school who had ridiculed me in the past would wander through the park. I would follow them, taunting them and call them names, trying to provoke a fight. On a few occasions they actually took the bait and fought and I usually won. But I was secretly angry at the people I was jealous of and this was still a very powerful force in my life. I was still very shy around girls and didn't know how to talk to them. This further-encouraged my aggression at those I did not like. I remember once in class at school there was another boy sitting in the class with me that I disliked intensely. He was one of those who teased and ridiculed me when I first started school. He was about my size too and I had always waited for the opportunity to get back at him. Well this day in class I finally had my chance. He made several derogatory comments (which weren't directed at me personally but rather at the recent invasion of Grenada by US forces) 'get out yanks.' I just stared at him from several chairs away with as much hostility as I could muster. A short while later our teacher briefly left the room for some reason and I stood up and walked over to this guy's chair. I had become so consumed with anger that I felt compelled to retaliate for this imagined slight. I didn't say anything, I just looked at him far a moment and then headbutted his head as hard as I could! It was totally unexpected and he almost burst into tears. All my friends in the class started laughing, everyone else was just silent. I stood there another second as if daring him to fight back, and when he didn't I laughed and walked back to my seat and sat down. The thing about this incident that bothers me most was that I'm sure he vividly remembers it that for no good reason I had humiliated him and for what? Making negative comments about the American government? I didn't even realize how wrong I was for quite some time. Although he had teased me in the early days I had done far worse to others since. Somewhere along the way I had actually become worse than the people I so hated. I had become the monster that I once feared. People respected me now but only because they feared me.

As I mentioned earlier my romantic/girlfriend situation could have been better. The only girls I actually knew were the ones who were dating my friends and I certainly wouldn't dream of trying to get involved with; There actually was one incident which taught me a lot about manipulation and sexual polities. One of the other skinheads was a guy named David who I never actually cared for much, and he was dating a very pretty girl named Valerie. She was always very friendly to me. In the beginning I think it was just a ploy to make David jealous but as time passed I thought she was really getting interested in me. The other girls would encourage drama by telling me she really liked me, I was so much nicer than David, etc, etc. Even with my fearsome reputation (which was about a year old by this time) I was still very naive when it comes to girls. But I did still have my values. Even though David wasn't exactly one of my favorite people he was still one of us so his girl was off limits, end of story. Valerie still continued to talk to me and flirt with me almost every day at the park. This flirtation was one sided because aside from my rule about friend's girlfriends I was also absolutely clueless on how to chat up a girl. The whole incident finally blew up one day when David walked up to us and began calling her a 'slag' and me a 'wanker.' She tried to calm him down and he violently pushed her away. This is when my serious flaw of 'mindless violence to make up for no sex life' reared its ugly head. To defend Valerie I basically attacked David and beat the shit out of him It wasn't difficult, he was drunk and I just happened to be sober at that point. The other skins just stood around and watched while I kicked David over and over again. While nowhere near as bad as what I done to McNabb it was still pretty bad. When I finished I stood over him while he lay curled up on the ground. I don't know what I expected, probably for Valerie to come running gratefully to my arms. What actually happened was Valerie called me a lot of names, burst into tears and then ran to David, cradling his head in her lap. I was completely at a loss.

The small smiles I saw on the other girls taught me all I would ever need to know about this silly drama.

More incidents were to follow. I continued to taunt, torment and terrorize those who I felt had wronged me somehow. Sometimes they deserved it, but usually they didn't. I was just an anger bully.

Any record of skinhead activities would be incomplete without politics and the racial question. I myself have never been a racist, personally I feel no one with any intelligence whatsoever can be a racist. But some of my friends did claim to follow Right Wing groups. They rarely acted on these impulses because most of us weren't racist and they needed us to back them for any cowardly attacks they wanted to do. It hadn't escaped my attention that people of colour avoided me like the plague. Although not racist myself I was treated as such which I detected in the reaction I got from people. I remember one time getting on a bus all decked out in bleached jeans, my boots, bomber jacket, shaved head and as I walked to the rear of the bus a mixed race woman grabbed her little girl who had been playing in the aisle and pulled her beside her, then held her close. I thought it was peculiar, until I realized she was scared. Scared of me. I was shocked. This woman who did not know me assumed I would hurt her child. So I sat as close to them as I could and went out of my way to make polite chit-chat, smile at the little girl, anything to put them at ease. I don't think it worked because when I got off the bus at my stop they still looked at me with fear. Hostile looks from non-white men didn't bother me, but looks of fear from women and children did. It bothered me a great deal. When the friends of mine who did have racist or Nazi sympathies made comments I would quickly challenge and remind them that I was much more of a foreigner than the West Indians and Pakistanis they claimed to hate so much. I made it clear their views were 'their views' but I didn't want to hear them. A lot of people assumed I was racist; for the most part I didn't care what they thought. I knew I wasn't - that was good enough for me.

When I was 17 years old two incidents happened that drove me away from the 'friends' I had made. I'd been a skinhead for about two years now and I had done a lot of stupid things. I'd been in many fights, was feared at school and I think now my mother longed for the 'good old days' when I was a pudgy, harmless 15 year old who whined about how awful England was. Now I smoked, drank a lot of beer and hung out with some scary looking people. But back to the incidents. It was a Saturday night in Reading and a famous psychobilly band was playing a concert'. Most of my friends, skins and psychobilly, were going but for whatever reason I didn't go. I was hanging out at Prospect Park the next day when I heard what had happened. One of the psychobillies had raped a girl at the show. The psychobilly in question was several years older than I was, very large and vary violent. In a twisted way I suppose we looked up to him as an accomplished thug and hooligan. On reflection it's strange when you see how you looked up to and respected some people for the wrong reasons. Anyway during the show at one point he was at the front of the crowd with only a girl between him and the barrier pole in front of the stage. The barrier pole came up to the girl's waist and when the crowd surged forward she was trapped partially bent over pole. She was wearing a short skirt. This huge psychobilly lifted her skirt, pulled her underpants aside and raped her. This was witnessed by several of my friends who were nearby. The girl was helpless and could do absolutely nothing to stop it. At one point the singer of the band (who assumed this to be a consensus act) even laughed, pointing at what was happening and made a joke. I heard this story from my friends the next day. A few made jokes like it was funny, others just nervously laughed along. I was horrified and disgusted. Not only had my 'friends' stood by and done nothing while a girl was raped, now they were laughing about it. I was so appalled and disgusted for even knowing these people I can't even truly explain it. I didn't know who the girl was and I don't even think it was ever reported, but I know it happened. I was so numb with shock I just walked away. I didn't know what to say. I went home and felt totally alone. I had no friends who weren't either skins or psychobilly and yet I could never feel the same way about them again. Even the decent ones who were repulsed went along with the laughter and jokes. In my mind they were almost as bad as the filthy animal that had raped the girl. As if I needed another wake-up call a short time later the second incident happened. Close to the park a murder took place. A guy I knew killed his girlfriend I knew them both, although not well. Ironically he was a psychobilly as well. The event was highly publicized because he had stabbed his girlfriend over and over again. The media grabbed onto him being a psychobilly and being a fanatic of music by 'The Meteors'. Once again I was shocked and disturbed by people I thought I knew. I just withdrew into myself. Although violent and very rebellious I still knew I was a good person deep inside. Yet people assumed I was a racist and treated me accordingly, people I had once liked thought rape was acceptable behaviour, and a guy I knew butchers his girlfriend. This wasn't me. I didn't even want to be associated with these people anymore. Would those 'friends' who laughed at rape think murder was funny too?! I didn't want to know. So I walked away from it all. School had just finished. I stopped returning phone calls and avoided all the places I used to hang out at. For all intents and purposes I dropped off the face of the earth as far as my friends were concerned. I had hung up my boots and wanted nothing more to do with any of it. The bullying, the pack mentality, the cowardly attacks. I wanted no more to do with 'friends' who did all these things and more. Once again I was alone.

A lot happened over the next year. I grew out my hair, stopped wearing 'skinhead clothes' and avoided any contact with my old friends. As school had just finished this was fairly easy to do. I got a job at a Waitrose supermarket not far from Stoneham school where I made a few friends. These new friends had no idea I'd ever been a skinhead or anything else about the last two years I was trying to forget. About this time I decided I wanted to enlist in the US military as soon as I turned 18. My father had recently retired from the Army and was living in England with us. My parents bought a nicer house on Cotswold Way and I started running and trying to take care of myself. Although I still loved the punk and Oi (shinhead) music that had initially been part of my attraction to the skinheads, which was the only part of that scene that I kept with me. My relationship with my parents had improved quite a bit although my brother and I still did not get along. Although I had long since outgrown my 'America is the answer to all problems' idea, I still wanted to go there and make my own life. The military seemed the obvious answer, and as a definite patriot I believed serving your country with at least one enlistment of military service was a must. I initially chose the army, because my father (a 23 year veteran of the Army) and also I'd grown up around it. He talked me out of it, basically saying I hated authority and would have a better chance in the Air Force. So I took the exam at Mildenhall Hall Air Force Base when I was 18 years old and requested 'Security Police' as a job. An odd choice I suppose since I had a history of hating authority and getting into a lot of minor trouble. But that was what interested me. I had one last Christmas at home with my family and friends in 1985. In January 1985 I enlisted in the United States Air Force and left England and all my anger behind.

Value Equals Anger

We attach a value to everything that we have in life from the paintwork on our car to the feelings that we have. For example you may feel very humiliated when someone makes a sarcastic remark towards you or about you, your country, your friends or whatever. The degree of how their comment has made you feel will determine the level of anger that you feel towards them. Yet if they were to direct that same comment or sarcasm towards me or in my direction it would probably provoke a grin, with me knowing that I am an expert in sarcasm myself and have the choice as to how I will react.

One thing I am certain of is that they do not have the power to switch me on like a tap or control my anger.

I am the one in control. Nobody is important enough to get to me.

I wasn't always like this. I wrote in my book 'Pre-emptive strikes' about how I punched out a squaddie at Colchester Zoo for the offensive remark that he made the birth mark on my daughters face. This attempt at getting a cheap laugh at my daughters expense was not a good move that day. I put a value on that of my family being made fun of and reacted accordingly. I don't think that I'm much different to anyone else when it comes to my loved ones, however these days I am much more aware of controlling my anger and will use my 'power to choose' my reaction 'wisely'.

I now realise that although I felt pretty down about an offensive remark to my daughter, how must she feel? From then on I set out to make her fully aware that she will be a target for some stupid people, so I have set out to desensitise her feelings to such comments in the future and also to train her as I do my adult students and my sons in how to deal with sarcasm.

All my kids now have the ability to put on offer their 'hot spots' and complexes before others get to them, so they can deal with it in a non upsetting or aggressive way. I have covered my method of doing this elsewhere in the book.

So I have spoken about the value that we put on being humiliated, but what about the paintwork on our car? Or the windows of our house? The area we live? The county we were born in?

The clothes we wear, or the tidiness of our home or office?

We attach a value to all of them and everything else that we have in life, and get really angry when someone devalues that.

Lets look at the car which may be your pride and joy which you polish every day, but you come out one morning to find that somebody has 'keyed it' and engraved a lovely comment about you in the gleaming paintwork.

How exactly do you think that they intend to profit by their actions? How do you think that they would like you to feel?

At a pretty good guess I would think it would be their intention to make you angry and cost you money! They are going to control you and switch you on!

So do you go along with that or find an alternative to your anger? I suggest that you pre-empt this person's actions way ahead of it even happening in the first place. I know one option may be to set up a C.C.T.V camera to record what is happening to your car if you fancy sitting there watching it all night like a saddo or you could just park in a garage or park the car elsewhere but at the end of the day its all unnecessary hassle.

My method or personal choice is to say

'I have a car with nice paintwork which I know will upset some people for whatever reasons and I know that my paintwork will get damaged and devalued. It's only a matter of time'

Accept that this is part of life and that of having nice things and it is going to happen sooner or later either by accident or intentional. Prepare for this just like you would a rainy day. Have you ever been shocked because it has rained? I would say no, maybe disappointed but not shocked that such a thing can happen because you know that sooner or later it is going to happen. It's all a state of mind, so why not apply this to the paintwork on your car and other things?

Sooner or later damage is going to happen! So prepare yourself for it mentally. Either make sure that you have the money put away for such an event happening or have it built into your insurance that they will cover such a situation with out hassle, fuss and penalizing you for criminal damage that is not your fault.

Gearing yourself up for events like this will definitely lessen your anger when the equivalent of the rainy day arrives.

Throughout my 15 years as a doorman I was always conscious of the fact that my car would be a target for any customer that I eject from the building. So I dealt with this by parking my car away from the venue and even bought myself an older car that I could use just for work because I expected it to get damaged. I was of the frame of mind that it is an eventuality that damage will occur and I just accepted it as part and parcel of having a car. The funny think was that because I expected it to happen every single week just as I do my numbers to come up on the lottery, my car never got vandalised or damaged. It always happened to the other doormen who would spend the entire night checking over their cars, shouting at customers for leaning on them or putting their glasses on the bonnet or roof.

It may not be the car that you apply a great value to. It could be something as simple as your nicely cared for garden which the neighbours cat shits in every day. To coin a phrase 'Shit happens!'

When you take time out and actually put some thought to what's happening you will realise that the cat has absolutely no understanding of what it is doing to you or the grief that its causing you by making you angry. This is not a problem that you can solve by talking to the cat or it's owner because at the end of the day the cat is not going to be able to understand logical debate or the way the world works. So you will have to find an alternative way to approach or deal with the problem and stop the cat using your garden as a toilet.

One option would be to get a dog as a deterrent but that in a way is still kind of using anger to deal with a problem because the dog will tear down the garden and attempt to harm the cat. You could buy a hi-tech cat scarer that will use a high-pitched noise or a visual display or a water spray to stop the cat from wanting to even enter your garden. How about becoming really extreme and getting your garden covered in wire mesh or put in short poles with strips of foil that will move with the slightest wind to scare the cat away. You could even ask the cat's owner if they will pay for someone to clear the crap from your garden on a daily basis! But whatever you do, don't just sit there day in and day out grinding your teeth getting angrier by the day each time it happens because it will happen. So sit up and accept that shit happens and then try to find a solution to it that will lessen the problem of you becoming angry every time that cat devalues your garden.

Lets change the scenario.

How about the window in your house getting broken either intentionally or by accident by someone. It has devalued the look and level of security of your home. So why not prepare for it?

Prepare in advance and have a spare pane of glass tucked away in the loft with a tub of putty or have some cash put away in an emergency fund for problems like this. Ok! You shouldn't have to do this because your window should not get broken; but when it does, you are going to have to initially buy and replace it anyway, so why not pre-empt that event and do it now. At least this way you will not get caught out after hours when all the shops are closed, forcing you to pay a fortune to an emergency glazier and possibly have a day off work as well to deal with it.

All that hassle over a simple pane of glass will certainly make your blood boil when you could just have easily prepared in advance at a tiny cost. If such a thing happened you will get great pleasure in knowing that you have prepared for it just like you would a rainy day. You will feel really good about yourself. Most of the time when we get angry at situations like this it's because you feel angry at being caught out unprepared for an emergency.

If you value something and are likely to be angered if somebody devalues it in some way, Pre-empt the event and experience by having a course of action, or way of rectifying matters as an alternative to being angry. I know one guy who devalued his ex partner's car with out even touching it so he could get rid of his anger at the fact that he was the one that had paid for it and was now skint. It was a car that he had always dreamed of getting whilst they were a couple but could not afford to due to paying the mortgage etc. When they split up she wanted to hurt him and one of the things that she did was to buy this particular car for herself with the money she received from his settlement. The car was a special model that you could not miss. She loved it when driving around town and everyone knew it was her and her new partner in it. This was the nearest she could get to being a celebrity. Although this car was a very special edition, this guy went out and bought the exact same model on the same plate and drove it around. Instead of anger he was now grinning at the fact that everyone would be looking into his car expecting to see his ex and her new partner, thinking it was their car. This guy would be there grinning back at the world knowing that every single person that looked in and thought it was his ex wife's car, would say to her. *'I thought I saw you today but when I look closer I saw....etc.'* The ex wife felt that she had been violated and that her car and celebrity status had been devalued.

So the situation of him being angry and her being happy had been reversed just by a duplicate car being bought.

I am not going to lay claim here that by taking any of these measures that you will rid yourself of anger completely, because it wont. But it will set you on the right path of managing or lessening the degree of your anger.

Anger Eats our Energy

A close friend of mine phoned me one day and said,

'Jamie, some guy has just ripped me off for around £12,000. I want him seen to, nothing too nasty-just enough to make him pay'

My reply was,

'Wohh! Slow down, let's have a chat about this and see what's happening. I can see you are very angry and upset, but there must be an alternative way to deal with this matter?'

I could hear in his voice and emotional state that he was really angry and upset. He was angry that he had trusted somebody and that they had let him down, he was also angry that he had been conned out of a lot of money, which left him feeling foolish. He was angry that he was bit of a lad himself yet his demands over the phone for his money had not been successful, which left him feeling weak. He was basically very angry!

He had been pondering over this day and night for over a week and had become run down and depressed about the whole matter. He had not eaten or slept properly, he had no energy, and felt exhausted and ill. For him to feel better again it would need me to go and beat the other guy up in order to get the money back. This was not the way to deal with it and I had to try and help my pal understand that there is an alternative to using violence.

I said to my pal,

'Do you realize how much energy this whole thing has drawn from you? You have wasted so much energy worrying over this problem, energy that you could have put to good use elsewhere and made twice the amount of money that you are worrying about'

I then told him to think of all the positive things that would not have happened if he had not met that guy, all the new contacts that he would not have which he obtained via the guy and of how many mistakes he can now avoid in the future due to this one experience.' Most important of all though; I tried to get through to him how much more he could have actually achieved had he put all that wasted energy to good use rather than wasting it by worrying and being angry. My friend paused and thought for a while and said to me,

'Jamie you know what? This is why I have phoned you because you always make me see sense and help me to look at things differently. I am going to go out today and hire myself a solicitor to chase up my money and just forget about it and get on with other business.'

Two weeks later my friend called me again about what had happened but this time he was buzzing with excitement and said,

'Jamie, I took your advice and put my energy to good use instead of just sitting around and letting it eat away at me. I've just had £10,000 of my money recovered by my solicitor at a cost of a few hundred pounds and in the meantime I've just pulled off a major contract worth thousands to me. Had I not spoken to you and taken your advice, I would have let my anger eat away at me and would still be £12,000 poorer. Also I would not have perused the avenues that led to the new contract that I have'

One happy ending!

So the moral of this true story is that the longer we remain in an angry state about something; the more our energy is literally drained away from us leaving us feeling weak and helpless. It's no different to putting a torch away but leaving it switched on even though it's not in use! It will drain the life out of the batteries and serve no purpose whatsoever. It makes much more sense to switch it off and only use the energy for something positive.

Anger will eat away at you and literally drain the life from you if you let it. I know only too well how much harm it can do to you if you let your anger eat away like a hungry vulture. I have been more guilty of this happening to me in the past than you can ever imagine and know only too well the result of allowing anger to eat away at me and steal all my energy. This condition has caused me to lose many things in my life due to my health and state of mind, things that didn't necessarily need to happen. However at the time I could not see myself from the outside or how I had become with my energy having being eaten away.

Thanks to this personal study on anger and its effect on us, I am able to put all that behind me now and leave it in the past. The torch has been switched off until I choose to switch it back on and I hope that my advice is going to be of help to you if you have suffered in this way or is going to help you, to help others.

If you see someone being angry and wasting their energy, try to help them see what they are doing to themselves especially if they are considering using the option of violence in any way.

Using your energy in a positive way has definitely got to be a better option than the anger vulture getting a grip of you and causing you to go around to break someone's legs or drain you into exhaustion. The violence option does not solve the reason that the person has become energy drained in the first place and it does nothing to help them manage their anger, eating away at their energy in the future.

Anger will only eat away at your energy if you let it. Anger will only treat you in the way that you allow it to!

Power to Choose

Stimulus and response, or action and reaction, happens with everything that we do in our lives, but there's something that's so important to us that it can make a big change to our lives. It certainly did with mine! This very important thing is called 'Space.'

It is the period of time that sits in-between our reaction to another's action. Some of us are aware of this period of space that sits between action and reaction because when we get angry about something, we stop ourselves exploding into a rage by counting to ten. This is a cool off period, which allows the flame in our fuse, time to go out.

What is actually happening here is that you are being given the 'power to choose' as to how you are going to react to a situation; be it with anger or without anger! Think carefully about what I am saying here.

You are actually being given a second chance as to how you are going to react to something when you first become angry. When I say second chance, I am basing this on the fact that you have not managed to stop yourself from becoming angry in the first place, so we are now into the realms of the cure rather than the prevention to your first stimulus provoking a reaction. This is where you now get a chance to distract, divert or get your mind focused on an alternative to anger. It may take a little more than just counting to ten to deal with your anger. For some people this method may be sufficient but for other they will find themselves just as angry as they were ten seconds before! Live radio chat shows and phone in's use this five to ten seconds delay to ensure that they have control over everything that they broadcast and it is within these vital few seconds that they have the power to choose what goes out to the listeners. They use that space wisely to make sure that the final choice is appropriate. You must use your power to choose what you do with your space and do it 'wisely.'

You have the power to choose, the words that come out of your mouth and the physical reaction that you will perform. Although counting to ten will be enough in itself for many people to deal with their reaction, for others it will only be sweeping it under the carpet; lift the carpet up and it's still there.

My advice is to remove yourself from the environment where the anger has occurred.

I know I've said this before but you can never give an important message too many times This is a method that I used a lot whilst working as a doorman. A situation would occur were someone had become angry because their drink had been knocked over or their partner was being chatted up; so they feel that they 'have' to act in an angry way; even more so if an audience if present! I would always ask the angered person to step into a quieter area of the club so that they could explain their problem to me. We would then have entered the 'space' period where they have the power to choose how they want to deal with their anger. I would then give them a few options of how they can resolve their anger without them feeling cowardly or belittled in front of their audience. It may even be the case that security will evict them from the club if they do kick off and do not calm their anger and cool off. Whatever alternative they have picked instead of letting their anger control them, it will be a decision that they are able to make away from the environment where the anger was first triggered off. They get to think logically in different surroundings where they are not having to act or think in a certain way to show off or please the spectators. Anger really is a spectator pastime.

Even if I were dealing with a situation where the person has a gripe with me because I have thrown out one of their mates for doing something wrong, I still deal with the matter in the same way. I would invite them to discuss the matter with me in a spectator free environment allowing them how to choose how they want to deal with their anger. I would say that on almost every occasion that the angry person would calm down and offer to shake my hand as a way of letting the problem disappear. I'm sure that a few of them have gone back to their mates and told them that they had given me a right 'Ticking off' in order for them to save face and look tough in front of their mates, but I wasn't bothered about that. I was happy with myself in being able to defuse a person's anger and I had not been forced to use violence as an option. It was done in a way that did not leave them feeling disempowered because it would give them the power to choose their response.

It would feel good to me if I had taken a serious anger situation and reduced the level of threat to simple anger and then on to no anger at all.

There were of course the odd occasions when the angered person were fuelled by excess alcohol or drugs which would not allow them to think logically or use the space in-between stimulus and repose wisely, where a serious situation of anger was heading in the direction of it becoming life threatening, well these people had to be dealt with differently. You can read about these situations in my book 'Thugs, Mugs and violence' because this book is not really looking at using violence as an option. What I will say though is that whether I had to talk someone down or knock them down, I was always happy with myself that I had allowed them to choose how they wanted to proceed with their feelings of anger. I would also always give myself a big pat on the back if I had defused a situation and saved somebody from getting glassed just because I had allowed another person the chance to choose an alternative to their anger.

So the most important message here is to immediately remove yourself, your family, you friends etc from the environment where anger has happened and use the space that sits in-between action and reaction wisely. Make use of your power to choose!

For a more in-depth look at dealing with environmental situations of anger turning to violence and how to cope with it, read my book 'Old School - New School' which will give you a behind the scenes insight as to how door supervisors and like deal with these situations.

Alternatives to Anger

What choices do we have instead of anger? Well apart from the dozens that there already are, there are many more! So we just have to find and use one that works for us.

For me personally, the happiness and smiles on the faces of my children, when I go to collect them for their weekly access visit to me, never fails to instantly wipe out any anger or upset that may creep into my life now and then. There was a time when I had lost my job, my money, my home, my family and had nothing more than the clothes on my back for a second time in my life and was at the end of my tether. I went and collected my children for the time that I had been granted by their mother and took them out for the day. My situation was so destitute that I had the choice of taking them out for an enjoyable day to the cinema, etc and not having any food money for myself for the week or sitting in a park in the pouring rain and saving my money. For me there was no choice. My children's happiness comes before I would even consider worrying about myself. Anyway on returning them back to their mother at the end of the day I was then going to leave them and go into stress mode about how shit my life was. Although their smiles and happiness would comfort me for the time we were together, I knew that this safety net would disappear when we were parted. When I dropped them home I knew that the dreaded time was about to arrive. That journey home alone where the angry wolves in my mind begin to attack me telling me how worthless I am as a human being and of how I have lost everything around me. Before I said my goodbyes to my children, my little girl gave me a big hug and a kiss and said to me

'Daddy, you really make my heart smile!'
That priceless little moment made me melt inside and made me realize how lucky I was to have children that

actually felt that way about me. I stopped being angry about all the things that had gone wrong for me because they were things that really didn't matter!

Sure I've been angry about different things since then but it's never been 'life threatening' as it was then back in the early days.

Although I feel embarrassed and ashamed at what a vulnerable person I once was, I have no choice but to admit on reflection as to how true it was. Anyway my whole point is that a few simple words from the right person at the right time, maybe all that's needed to wipe away any anger that you have and will enable you to get your whole life back on track. For those lucky enough to have their children living with them full time; a few simple words like those I received from my little girl might not mean as much because you see them daily and may not have the same effect. You are more likely to be worried about the mud they have walked onto your carpet or the milk they have left out of the fridge. If that is the case then you will need to find something else that's special to you in order to wipe out or work as an alternative to your anger. Some find it in caring words from a partner, friend or family.

Some people find it helpful to work out on a punch bag, others go jogging or do an aerobic workout and some even use alcohol or drugs to deal with their anger. Whatever choice you make it must be the lesser of the two evils. Alcohol and drugs are not a good option but if either of them stops you from caving in another person's skull then it must be the lesser of the two evils. However it serves no purpose ridding yourself of anger if you end up a Heroin addict, just as there is no point in getting drunk and fighting in pubs to get rid of your anger. I was told once of one couple who had a male and female ornamental penguin on display which would be turned back to back when one of them were unhappy with the other. What a brilliant alternative to anger that is, opposed to going a few rounds of verbal abuse with each other.

When I was in the business of being paid to sort out other people's grievances, it was mostly from people that would get rid of their anger by paying me to collect money that was owed to them. That is how they managed to get rid of their anger, by paying a price for a problem to be dealt with, by me. Be it right or wrong that's what worked for them. One lady paid someone else I knew to go around and deal with the attackers who abused her daughter because the police were not dealing with it as she saw fit.

If she had not paid to release herself of how angry she felt at the attackers, and at the police, then she would be carrying that baggage around for the rest of her days had she not found another way of dealing with it. Her way of dealing with matters may not be legal or orthodox but it's what worked for her and she was prepared to also pay the price of going to prison herself had it come to it. I am not suggesting that the alternative to anger is revenge, because its not! But many people will always deal with matters in this way until they are able to find better alternatives. Alternatives will differ, depending on what it is that has made you angry in the first place and to what degree of anger you are suffering, be it simple, serious or life threatening.

Here are some things for you to try;

1. Make a list detailing ways that you have rid yourself of anger in the past?

2. Make a list of methods that you know other people have used which has worked for them?

3. List some possibilities and alternatives to anger that you would advise friends and family to use rather than anger eating away at them?

4. Analyse yourself and try to find out why you can suggest certain alternatives to others to deal with their anger, yet you are not able to use them yourself.

5. Write down any anger alternatives that you may have used in the past, which haven't worked and try to work out why they failed. See if a different alternative or approach may have been more suitable.

6. Take a good look at yourself and decide if you are an anger bully but may not have realised it before? If so what are you going to do about it?

Respect Me or Else!

It's not much to ask for, a little respect! It's something we all want isn't it! In some shape or form we all want to be respected don't we? Here's a little story about respect.

A young lad of 18 once told me that he respected four people who stood for everything that he wanted to be in life. These people were American musical artists Eminem aka Slim Shady, Tu Pac, Notorious B.I.G, and little old English me?

I did not understand the comparison? Three American gangsta rappers and one fat bloke from East London (Me). His idea of the common trait that we all had was that we were all respected by people that wanted to be hard. He had this false impression in his head that I was some sort of a gangster that had beaten, tortured, and killed people to gain respect for myself. All utter crap of course. I explained to him that I have used hard work and friendship to gain people's respect and have not done it through using anger and violence. Sure, I use controlled violence when teaching people self protection and part and parcel of that teaching is to show others how to use, maim or kill another human being if necessary for their survival; I have also spent over a decade working as a doorman dealing with thousands of violent confrontations and throughout my 40 years on this earth I have had hundreds of successful street fights, so I can see where he may be getting this false impression from. However he has never seen me in any violent type of fight or encounter so it is definitely something that he has falsely created within his own mind as to why he thinks people respect me. Although I would not think twice about coming through your door at 5am and beating you to a pulp before you could even wipe the sleep from your eyes, if you harmed one of my children. I would not gain any respect for that. That kind of thing sickens people and makes them not want to be around you through fear that they may one day upset you. That gains disrespect – not respect!

I had to explain to this lad that I gained my respect through being a true and honest person. I detest violence, bullying, and seeing anybody suffer. This lad had the complete wrong idea as to why people supposedly respected me.

He wanted me to be a 'tough guy' that he could emulate and that really sickened me. He wanted to go out and hurt people, stab people, and kill people just to release his anger at not being respected. He wanted to be like me, Tu Pac, BIG, and Slim Shady so that he could be respected as we all were, be it for different reasons. He really believed that it would make people respect him!

His problem was that he was really angry at not yet having found that one special thing that he is good at. We are all good at something but just need to explore from life as much as we can that's available to us until we find it. I did not know I could write a book until I was 36 and I now have six books out. He has not put any time into exploring what it is that makes him different. He may find it tomorrow or it may take years, but if he doesn't try he will forever be angry.

Nobody respected me when I was a door-to-door 'Spy-hole' salesman, or a manager in a Dog food factory because I was just the same as everybody else out there. I had to find a way in which I was different and then set out to exploit that so as to get on in life.

I could have turned to drugs, crime and mindless violence as many of my friends did but that was too easy. It would have made me just the same as the rest of them. To be different I refused to smoke or have tattoos done or take part in football violence like the rest of the lads because that would also make me just the same.

To get real genuine respect I had to be different and not gain a false sense of respect through making people fear me as my friends made others fear them. People who respect you through fear will dance on your grave the second your gone, but those that genuinely respect you will respect you forever or until you mess up.

The message that I was trying to get through to this young lad was that if he really wanted to be respected by people then he will have to earn that respect by being different and not just other wannabe 'gangsta rappa' into drugs and violence.

I can take him to any street in any city and show him dozens of kids all promoting drugs and violence as a way to gain respect. If that is the route that he wants to take then he will always be a nobody, dressing like them, walking and talking like them and may even end up dead as his heroes Tu Pac & the Notorious B.I.G.

Yet on the other hand if he searched the whole country he would still only find one like 'me' because I'm different and have gained my respect from being different.

I gave this lad my book 'Thugs, mugs & violence' and asked him to go read it to see if he could learn something different about how to gain respect, then come back to me and tell me if his respect for me is different to that he has for the gangsta rappers and why?

He phoned me recently and said that I had inspired him to do something with his life and he realised that he needs to be different. He has even begun writing a book. So how's that for a turnaround!

I hope from this tale you will be able to help other youngsters to understand why they are being angry. That being that they are not getting the respect that they desire. Hopefully you can show them an alternative route to gaining respect for themselves in a way that will show the world how they are different. Remind them that what they cannot be today – they can be tomorrow. But only if they are different to the masses.

Quotes on Anger

Usually when people are sad, they don't do anything. They just cry over their condition. But when they get angry, they bring about a change.
Malcolm X
1925-1965, American Black Leader, Activist

Anyone can become angry -- that is easy. But to be angry with the right person, to the right degree, at the right time, for the right purpose, and in the right way -- this is not easy.
Aristotle
BC 384-322, Greek Philosopher

We praise a man who feels angry on the right grounds and against the right persons and also in the right manner at the right moment and for the right length of time.
Aristotle
BC 384-322, Greek Philosopher

Never forget what a person says to you when they are angry.
Henry Ward Beecher
1813-1887, American Preacher, Orator, Writer

Speak when you are angry and you will make the best speech you will ever regret.
Ambrose Bierce 1842-1914, American Author, Editor, Journalist, "The Devil's Dictionary"

No person is important enough to make me angry.
Carlos Castaneda
American Anthropologist, Author

An angry man opens his mouth and shuts his eyes.
Cato The Elder   BC 234-149, Roman Statesman, Orator

I know of no more disagreeable situation than to be left feeling generally angry without anybody in particular to be angry at.
Frank Moore Colby
1865-1925, American Editor, Essayist

Never go to bed angry, stay up and fight.
Phyllis Diller
1861-1951, American Columnist

For every minute you are angry you lose sixty seconds of happiness.
Ralph Waldo Emerson
1803-1882, American Poet, Essayist

Whenever you are angry, be assured that it is not only a present evil, but that you have increased a habit.
Epictetus
50-120, Stoic Philosopher

Two things a man should never be angry at: what he can help, and what he cannot help.
Thomas Fuller
1608-1661, British Clergyman, Author

When I am right, I get angry. Churchill gets angry when he is wrong. So we were often angry at each other.
Charles De Gaulle
1890-1970, French President during World War II

If a small thing has the power to make you angry, does that not indicate something about your size?
Sidney J. Harris
1917-American Journalist

When angry, count to ten before you speak. If very angry, count to one hundred.
Thomas Jefferson 1743-1826, Third President of the USA

When I am angry I can pray well and preach well.
Martin Luther
1483-1546, German Leader of the Protestant Reformation

The angry man will defeat himself in battle as well as in life.
Samurai Maxim

Every time you get angry, you poison your own system.
Alfred A. Montapert
American Author

No one is as angry as the person who is wrong.
Proverb

An angry man is again angry with himself when he returns to reason.
Publilius Syrus
1st Century BC, Roman Writer

When angry, count four; when very angry, swear.
Mark Twain
1835-1910, American Humorist, Writer

The size of a man is measured by the size of the thing that makes him angry.
Source Unknown

No one can make us angry. People can say and do things to us but it is still up to us as individuals to do what we want with our emotions in response to those things.
Source Unknown

The broad general rule is that a man is about as big as the things that make him angry.
Source Unknown

Events will take their course, it is no good of being angry at them; he is happiest who wisely turns them to the best account.

Euripides
BC 480-406, Greek Tragic Poet

Every man who attacks my belief, diminishes in some degree my confidence in it, and therefore makes me uneasy; and I am angry with him who makes me uneasy.

Samuel Johnson
1709-1784, British Author

Change hurts. It makes people insecure, confused, and angry. People want things to be the same as they've always been, because that makes life easier. But, if you're a leader, you can't let your people hang on to the past.

Richard Marcinko
American Business Author

Nothing makes people so worthy of compliments as receiving them. One is more delightful for being told one is delightful -- just as one is more angry for being told one is angry.

Katherine F. Gerould

One lesson we learn early, that in spite of seeming difference, men are all of one pattern. We readily assume this with our mates, and are disappointed and angry if we find that we are premature, and that their watches are slower than ours. In fact, the only sin which we never forgive in each other is difference of opinion.

Ralph Waldo Emerson 1803-1882, American Poet, Essayist

No one can make you jealous, angry, vengeful, or greedy -- unless you let him.

Napoleon Hill
1883-1970, American Speaker, Motivational Writer, 'Think and Grow Rich'

It is easy to fly into a passion... anybody can do that, but to be angry with the right person to the right extent and at the right time and in the right way... that is not easy.

Aristotle
BC 384-322, Greek Philosopher

Envy among other ingredients has a mixture of the love of justice in it. We are more angry at undeserved than at deserved good-fortune.

William Hazlitt
1778-1830, British Essayist

It is dangerous to let the public behind the scenes. They are easily disillusioned and then they are angry with you, for it was the illusion they loved.

W. Somerset Maugham
1874-1965, British Novelist, Playwright
An angry father is most cruel toward himself.

Publilius Syrus
1st Century BC, Roman Writer

To be angry is to revenge the faults of others on ourselves.

Alexander Pope
1688-1744, British Poet, Critic, Translator

He that will be angry for anything will be angry for nothing.

Sallust
BC 86-34, Roman Historian

In the beginning the Universe was created. This has made a lot of people very angry and has been widely regarded as a bad move.

Douglas Adams
1952-, British Science Fiction Writer

Be not angry that you cannot make another what you wish them to be; since you cannot make yourself what you wish to be.

Thomas ã Kempis
1379-1471, German Monk, Mystic, Religious Writer

You are not angry with people when you laugh at them. Humour teaches tolerance.

W. Somerset Maugham
1874-1965, British Novelist, Playwright

Try as much as possible to be wholly alive, with all your might, and when you laugh, laugh like hell and when you get angry, get good and angry. Try to be alive. You will be dead soon enough.

William Saroyan
1908-1981, American Writer, Novelist,, Playwright

When a man is wrong and won't admit it, he always gets angry.

Thomas C. Haliburton
1796-1865, Canadian Jurist, Author

Angry people need to criticize as an outlet for their anger. That's why you must reject unkind criticism. Unkind criticism is never part of a meaningful critique of you. Its purpose is not to teach or to help, its purpose is to punish. Life isn't supposed to be an all or nothing battle between misery and bliss. Life isn't supposed to be a battle at all.

Barbara Sher
American Author of 'I Could Do Anything If I Only Knew What It Was'

I was angry with my friend: I told my wrath, my wrath did end. I was angry with my foe: I told it not, my wrath did grow.

William Blake
1757-1827, British Poet, Painter

Sticks and stones are hard on bones aimed with angry art.
Words can sting like anything but silence breaks the heart.
Phyllis McGinley
1905-1978, American Poet, Author

A large part of mankind is angry not with the sins, but with the sinners.
Seneca 4 B.C. – 65 A.D., Spanish-born Roman Statesman, philosopher

Travelers are like poets. They are mostly an angry race.
Sir Richard Burton
1821-1890, Explorer, Born in Torquay

There must be a reason why some people can afford to live well. They must have worked for it. I only feel angry when I see waste. When I see people throwing away things that we could use.
Mother Teresa
1910-1997, Albanian-born Roman Catholic Missionary

A man would prefer to come home to an unmade bed and a happy woman than to a neatly made bed and an angry woman.
Marlene Dietrich
1904-1992, German-born American Film Actor

Indulge not thyself in the passion of anger; it is whetting a sword to wound thine own breast, or murder thy friend.
Akhenaton
BC -~1375, Egyptian King, Monotheist

I used to store my anger and it affected my play. Now I get it out. I'm never rude to my playing partner. I'm very focused on the ball. Then it's over.
Helen Alfredsson
American Golfer

The more anger towards the past you carry in your heart, the less capable you are of loving in the present.

Barbara De Angelis
American Expert on Relationship & Love, Author

Bitterness is like cancer. It eats upon the host. But anger is like fire. It burns it all clean.

Maya Angelou
1928-, African-American poet, Writer, Performer

Consider how much more you often suffer from your anger and grief, than from those very things for which you are angry and grieved.

Marcus Antonius
c.83-30 BC, Roman Triumvir, Related to Julius Caesar

How much more grievous are the consequences of anger than the causes of it.

Marcus Aurelius
121-80 AD, Roman Emperor, Philosopher

Anger cannot be dishonest.

George R. Bach

Anger makes dull men witty -- but it keeps them poor.

Francis Bacon
1561-1626, British Philosopher, Essayist, Statesman

Holding on to anger is like grasping a hot coal with the intent of throwing it at someone else; you are the one getting burned.
Buddha
568-488 BC, Founder of Buddhism

You will not be punished for your anger, you will be punished by your anger.
Buddha   568-488 BC, Founder of Buddhism

Anger will never disappear so long as thoughts of resentment are cherished in the mind. Anger will disappear just as soon as thoughts of resentment are forgotten. Buddha
568-488 BC, Founder of Buddhism

Anger ventilated often hurries towards forgiveness; anger concealed often hardens into revenge.

Edward G. Bulwer-Lytton
1803-1873, British Novelist, Poet

In a controversy the instant we feel anger we have already ceased striving for the truth, and have begun striving for ourselves.

Thomas Carlyle
1795-1881, Scottish Philosopher, Author

Anger is the most impotent of passions. It effects nothing it goes about, and hurts the one who is possessed by it more than the one against whom it is directed.

Clarendon

The intoxication of anger, like that of the grape, shows us to others, but hides us from ourselves.

Charles Caleb Colton
1780-1832, British Sportsman Writer

When anger rises, think of the consequences.

Confucius
BC 551-479, Chinese Ethical Teacher, Philosopher

Anger, even when it punishes the faults of delinquents, ought not to precede reason as its mistress, but attend as a handmaid at the back of reason, to come to the front when bidden. For once it begins to take control of the mind, it calls just what it does cruelly.

George William Curtis
1824-1892, American Journalist

He who holds back rising anger like a rolling chariot, him I call a real driver; other people are but holding the reins

Dhammapada
BC 300-, Buddhist Collection of Moral Aphorism

There's nothing wrong with anger provided you use it constructively.
Wayne Dyer
1940-, American Psychotherapist, Author, Lecturer

To rule one's anger is well; to prevent it is better.
Tryon Edwards
1809-1894, American Theologian

There was never an angry man that thought his anger unjust.
St. Francis De Sales
1567-1622, Roman Catholic Bishop, Writer

Whatever is begun in anger, ends in shame.
Benjamin Franklin
1706-1790, American Scientist, Publisher, Diplomat

Anger and intolerance are the twin enemies of correct understanding.
Mahatma Gandhi
1869-1948, Indian Political, Spiritual Leader

Anger is an expensive luxury in which only men of a certain income can indulge.
St. Gregory The Great
c. 540-604, Italian Pope

Anger is never without an argument, but seldom with a good one.
Edward F. Halifax
1881-1959, British Conservative Statesman

Anger is a momentary madness, so control your passion or it will control you.

Horace
BC 65-8, Italian Poet

Anger is a brief lunacy.

Horace
BC 65-8, Italian Poet

The one who cannot restrain their anger will wish undone, what their temper and irritation prompted them to do.

Horace
BC 65-8, Italian Poet

Anger is short madness
Horace

Anger blows out the lamp of the mind. In the examination of a great and important question, everyone should be serene, slow-pulsed and calm.

Robert Green Ingersoll
1833-1899, American Orator, Lawyer

He who is slow to anger has great understanding, but he who has a hasty temper exalts folly.

Proverb

If you are patient in one moment of anger, you will escape a hundred days of sorrow.

Chinese Proverb

Beware of him that is slow to anger; for when it is long coming, it is the stronger when it comes, and the longer kept. Abused patience turns to fury.

Francis Quarles
1592-1644, British Poet

Man should forget his anger before he lies down to sleep.
Thomas De Quincey
1785-1859, British Author

The anger of a person who is strong, can always bide its time.
John Ruskin
1819-1900, British Critic, Social Theorist

The deferring of anger is the best antidote to anger.
Seneca
4 B.C. – 65 A.D., Spanish-born Roman Statesman,
philosopher

Anger is like those ruins, which smash themselves on what they fall.
Seneca   4 B.C. – 65 A.D., Spanish-born Roman Statesman,
philosopher

Anger: an acid that can do more harm to the vessel in which it is stored than to anything on which it is poured.
Seneca
4 B.C. – 65 A.D., Spanish-born Roman Statesman,
philosopher

The greatest remedy for anger is delay.
Seneca 4 B.C. – 65 A.D., Spanish-born Roman Statesman,
Philosopher

Anger is a great force. If you control it, it can be transmuted into a power, which can move the whole world.
Sri Swami Sivananda
1887-, Indian Physician, Sage

Let us not look back in anger or forward in fear, but around in awareness.

James Thurber
1894-1961, American Humorist, Illustrator

Keep cool; anger is not an argument.

Daniel Webster
1782-1852, American Lawyer, Statesman

There is not in nature, a thing that makes man so deformed, so beastly, as doth intemperate anger.

John Webster
1580-1625, British Dramatist

Don't look back in anger
Noel Gallagher - Oasis

There is only a hairline difference that separates Danger from anger and that is the letter D. Anger and Danger are closer than you ever realized.

Jamie O'Keefe

Beyond our Control

I will begin here by describing an experience that is pretty common to us all, be it in different scenarios but it will still include all the same ingredients.

One day I made a promise to my daughter that I will collect her from her mothers at 10.00 on Saturday morning to get her to her dancing competition which she had spent six months training for. My employer at that time informed me that I were to hand over the office, safe and car keys to his driver at 08.00 because he was at the airport and had forgotten some documents which were in his house. At 08.30 the driver had still not arrived so I was becoming a little anxious about getting away to collect my daughter. I tried phoning my employer but his mobile was switched off and by 09.00 I'm pretty

angry. I'm really starting to panic that I am not going to be in time to collect my daughter. When I finally manage to get through to my employer he informs me that his cleaner was at his house that day so he redirected his driver there to collect the items that he needed and now had them in his possession. Throughout the whole process nobody had thought to contact me to say I need not wait around, so by now I am really pissed off and angry.

My promise to my daughter at this moment in time is more important than any job or my respect or attitude towards my employer. All I could think about was getting to my daughter by 10.00.

I now rush out to my car and tear down the road like a madman only to realise I am almost out of fuel and the gauge is showing red.. Shit!!!

I pull into the next available garage and find the fuel pumps to be of the old type and the nozzle will not fit into my unleaded tank. I am now tearing my hair out and screaming at the poor petrol attendant, who is getting the anger that I picked up at my last stop, that being work! So as I drive angrily out of the garage I almost have an accident and cause unintentional road rage to another driver. He is rightly upset with my driving and flashes his headlights at me so I rapidly show him the middle finger. This poor driver has now collected the anger I picked up at work and at the petrol garage.

I now make my way to the next garage and get my fuel but as I'm waiting to pay the queue is being held up by somebody asking directions to somewhere but they need it explained to them at least three times because they are too tight to buy a map guide of the area.

I now become verbally aggressive with this guy and the attendant and unleash my anger that I collected at the last three stops. It's now 09.30 and I am late.

There is no way that it is now physically possible for me to reach and collect my daughter by 10.00. I am now angry with myself for letting her down. So I arrive late for my daughter who is waiting at the door with her irate mother who screams out the obvious *'You're late'* progressing on to inform me what a waste of space I am as a father, and of how her current partner would have got my daughter to dancing on time. I react by informing my ex wife of all the imperfections that she has along with a few more that I just made up on the spot due to being so angry. My daughter then gets into my car crying at having witnessed her parents bawling at each other

and I tear down the road like a getaway driver to get her to the show on time. She arrives in a distressed state; messes up her routine through not being able to concentrate and returns back home, never wanting to go dancing again. This whole drama began at 08.00 in the morning and could have been totally avoided had I dealt with the key and employer situation differently. I'm sure that situations like this which have a knock on effect are all too familiar to you. Looking at this example, how could things have been different?

Have a think about similar scenarios where you have felt that you have ended up angry due to something that you felt was beyond your control and backtrack the chain of events to see if the whole thing could have been dealt with differently. It may only need one or two tiny ways of dealing with matters to turn you day into an anger free one.

'I'm late, I'm late, for a very important date'
from Alice In Wonderland.

Is that how things are for you? If you plan for things that may be beyond your control then you may be able to avoid problems that have made you angry in the past!

Control Freaks Get Angry

The control freak is really someone that I try to avoid in my life. I do not like being controlled or having people trying to control me. I do not need anybody telling me how I need to live my life. I'm big enough to be able to work that out for myself. I find it quite sad when somebody suddenly takes it upon themselves to organise my life for me; unless I have specifically asked for their advice and help. Opinion and advice I can handle but as for being 'told' how to conduct my life? No thanks!

Using the work 'Freaks' is probably not the best choice of words within the world of political correctness, but it is a word that we do use and is in context with the subject matter. Now for some strange reason, control freaks seem to take it really personally when they come across the likes of me.

They find it really hard to accept when people do not want to be controlled by them. Well excuse me folks but if they want to be a pack leader then they may be better off buying themselves an obedient puppy with witch they can play the power and control game. This is not just a male problem, however I have seen a lot of it in abusive relationships. Men are more into the power and control bullshit but don't let that fool you because females are just as good at it when it comes to taking charge of things. I've worked with quite a few real hardened doormen over the years who still hide away from the verbal onslaught of their partners because they just cannot handle it when their partners kick off.

I am the first to hold my hands up and admit that I'm guilty of being a control freak in my past life but this was due to of my fear of being cheated on, which was the thing that caused me to be like that in the first place, but I have my mind and life pretty balanced now. It took me a long time to rid myself of the control freak attributes and I am now a much better person for it. So that is another branch from the old anger tree that I am able to break off and do away with. Have you maybe begun to recognise any of the control freak attributes within yourself?

Ask yourself!

1. Do I try to get others to do something that I want them to do, rather than it being something that they personally decided to do through choice?

2. Do you try pressurizing people into doing things?

If your answer to these questions is yes, then it is very likely that you also get angry with others when they are not prepared to be controlled by you.

Do you feel inferior and weak when you cannot control, resulting in anger? Well why don't you stop yourself from becoming angry by stopping yourself from trying to take control of other peoples lives. Its quite simple really when you think about it. It took me quite some time to sort myself out but the journey was worthwhile!

We can also look at the control thing from another perspective. That being when someone is trying to control you! Are you going to accept it or are you going to stand up for yourself and deal with it? People will only treat you in the way that you allow them to and control freaks just love to treat you as if they are in charge of you! Letting this happen will leave you with an uncomfortable sickly feeling for the rest of your life unless you are prepared to meet it head on. Stand up for yourself and they will be angry with you for a short while but this dreaded few minutes or even seconds will make a change in the way you feel for the rest of your life. Is feeling weak and controlled for the rest of your life a better option than feeling weak and scared for a few seconds? I don't think so! Another thing to consider here is that many control freaks do not even realize that they are trying to be so controlling over you. So do yourself and them a favour and make them aware of how they are conducting themselves.

I personally have no problem myself in letting someone know that I feel that they are trying to control and even bully me. Having been a former control freak, I am fully able to spot members of the 'Control Freak Club' so its easy for me to educate them a little about having a day off now and then from being a pain in the arse. You may not find it so easy to detect or deal with but the rule of thumb here is that if you are being made to feel helpless, then someone else may possibly be controlling you. In my more aggressive prior life I have often reacted to being controlled by someone with *'Who the fuck do you think you are my father?'* and this in turn often led to a fully blown argument. These days I am more inclined to say something like

' Look I know you have my interest at heart but I would be grateful if you give me the option or choice to make up my own mind and have my own experiences, this way I will be fully responsible for the consequences of my actions'

This will hopefully make them realise how they are acting and will give them the option to back off without losing face. The result being, no loss of face, no anger!

If they are the type of person that you are not going to change or stop, no matter how nicely you try and deal with it, then exclude them from your future as much as you are able, BUT tell them why you are doing so! They will still then have the chance to change their ways if they want you in their lives.

My stepfather became a very angry man when I as a young lad ever tried to challenge his power and control over me. So at the age of 26 I felt it was time for me to stand my ground, but this made him angry; so much so that it made him try to enforce even more power and control over my mother, my sister and me. Also because one of us was challenging him, he felt that he had to set an example towards all of us. I came to realise that I was not going to be able to make change in him because his control attributes had been caste in stone for over 50 years and acted out through habit. My only option was to take myself out of his life and also deny him the option of seeing my children grow. This lasted for over a year, but it took this to stop him acting this way towards me. As hard as it must have been for him to accept that he needed to change his angry and bullying ways, he did it as best as he possibly could. We then had a few great anger and control free years together before he died.

But if I had not taken that year of control away from him - he would have spent his last few years bitter and angry. I know that I helped make a change.

You do have a choice with dealing with control freaks. You can put up with their domineering attitude which will make you feel angry, or you can put a stop to it and this will probably leave them angry.

I know which I prefer! Other words that you could use for 'control freak' is 'anger bully' especially within a relationship. It seems to me that we are in a society when everyone wants to be in control from parental control to politics.

If you want to lead in life rather than be led. Do it in a way that is acceptable to those that you want it to mater to. Don't try to control people because that will only make you disliked. You may even already be doing it to others already without even realising it. Are you like that? Think about it?

Do you get angry when people do not do what you want them to do?

You may be a control freak and not even realise it! Cure this problem if it exists and you will rid yourself of some more anger!

Conditional Love and Anger

I spent the last 20 years of my life dealing with a mother and sister that I barely recognised due to an addiction problem that they both had. My mother was an alcoholic and my sister addicted to drugs. It would anger me so much that they would be under the influence of their own forms of drug from when they got up in the morning until their body collapsed in it's intoxicated state by the end of the day. It has been longer than I can ever remember when I was able to have a normal conversation with either of them not being under the influence of something.

A phone call from either of them to see how my children or I were getting on was a rare event. The same went for visits to my home. They were both forced into a situation of selfishness that forced them to think of themselves from the very moment they got up due to the very first thing on either of their minds was to get their first fix of alcohol or drugs. This went before everything and everyone in life, yet I still loved them both to death.

I can remember back to when I went away for a year and left them in possession of my keys to my flat so that my home and mail could be checked on regularly and they could update me when they visited me or I was able to phone them. I was always informed that all was ok but when I returned home after my year was up I returned to find my home had been cleared of all my furniture and belongings and anything tradable that could be sold, was! I had apparently been broken into but strangely enough the front door was intact. My family tried to convince me that somebody must have broken into the flat via the rear window and taken everything out that way. The snag with that story was that I lived four floors up in a tower block!

I did not involve the police because it was obvious that it was an inside job and it would amount to my own family getting arrested. As angry as I was about the whole matter, I loved them too much to bother myself with it.

I discovered over time that people became angry with those that they love when they put conditions on what they have to do in order to receive, deserve or gain that love from them. Love should not be conditional with your family. You should never say or think that you will only love a family member if they do something or act in a certain way. That's not how true love works. Love should always be unconditional, so in my situation where my home contents had been sold, I still found it in me to love my family. Ok! I was angry and upset at my possessions being sold by my own family but I knew deep down that it was not because they did not love me. It was because they both had addictive illnesses. Had they given me the option and whether they would steal from me or from a stranger, I would have chosen me! Given the option of them stealing from a stranger and getting caught, getting beaten up, getting sent to prison 'or' stealing from me and none of this happening to them.... The choice is an easy one, well for me anyway! Over the last 20 years my mother and sister have hurt me inside more than they could ever have envisaged due to the way their addictive illnesses have forced them to live their lives, but never once has this changed the unconditional love that I have for both of them. No matter how many times I phone them to make sure that they are o.k. it was guaranteed that they would rush me off the phone because they need to get on with things that are more important to them than me, yet I still never gave up. In the early days I would get angry but came to realise that anger would change nothing. They could not help the way they were due to their individual illnesses. I have at times put down the phone with a lump in my throat and tears rolling down my face after calling my mother but she had been so drunk that she did not even know who I was.

After the death of my Stepfather hit me badly some years ago, I thought to myself that although it angered me everytime I call my mother to find her drunk and not able to hold a sentence together, at least I was still able to hear her voice every day which made me luckier than some. I came to the conclusion that I would rather have a drunken mother who was doing what she was happy doing in her daily life than have a sober mother who was no longer alive as my stepfather; so what was the point in getting angry when I was getting the choice that I wanted?

I also realised that the reason that my mother and sister were able to see and speak to each other daily and never get angry with each other was because they both accepted each other for the way they were, warts and all.

They both had addictions and accepted that in each other so were able to love each other unconditionally, ignoring all else. This was something that took me a long time to get to grips with because I was judgemental about the way they chose to lead there lives, or in my opinion waste their lives.

However it never made any change to the love I had for them – that was unconditional, so it was only the anger thing that I had to get under control. I eventually decided that if I phoned either of them and they were under the influence of drink or drugs I would simply say to them,

'I don't think its a suitable time to speak to you because I do not think you are able to concentrate right now so I will call you tomorrow.'

There was no anger or bad feeling on my part and allowed me to come away from the call, calm and not angry. It was my alternative to *' Your drunk aren't you'*

'No I'm not I haven't had a drink at all today'

'Yes you have I can hear you slurring' etc… That route always guaranteed that I would come away angry and it still wouldn't change anything!

I had to accept that, this was the way they chose to lead their lives and probably always will do, so my love had to be unconditional if I am to accept their lifestyle and rid myself of my anger.

Have a think about your own personal life and if you are applying conditional love to a member of your family, which is causing you to become angry with them when they do not comply to how you 'prefer' them to live. True love should be unconditional. Only when you are able to accept and apply this are you going to be able to stop yourself becoming angry within this area of your life. Applying unconditional love is not always going to be easy with some family members and I cannot guarantee that it is going to be possible for every one, but one thing I do know is that there is no reason that you are not able to give it a good try. So if you want to try and rid yourself of anger within the family arena then try tomorrow what you haven't tried before. For me friends are a different matter. I care for my friends but love is not a term that comes to mind, I do not come from that school of thought.

You can pick your friends but you cannot pick your family. So for friends I use some of the other methods within this book where I would replace the word 'Love' with the word 'Care.'

Prior to my mother's unexpected death in September 2000 I had already scrapped this book and decided to not release it due to legal reasons forbidding me to include a few chapters that I personally felt were important to the book. As I awaited the funeral of my mother I sat and read back through to see if I had made any comments that I now felt different about on reflection considering the sudden change in my circumstances and reorganisation of my life. I still had no intention of releasing the book but after reading through the piece on unconditional love and anger, I felt this is a worthwhile publication for this advice alone and have not changed this piece in any way.

So thank you mum for bringing this book back from the scrap heap. This book was completed and finished on Mothers Day 25th March 2001 in remembrance of my dear mother.

Types of Aggression

Territorial Aggression

Throughout time there has be numerous cases of people being maimed or killed just for being in the wrong place at the wrong time. Their only crime was to step into another person's space or area whether or not they realised that they had done so. Well it is this type of aggression, which is known as 'territorial aggression' that stops us from over populating areas. We all need our own space and it is proven that the more built up an area is and the more that people are infringing on each other's space - Anger rears itself much more often. Too many people within an unsuitable amount of space will put a strain on the amount of resources that are available because there is only a certain amount of anything to go around, be it seats, food, water, beach area, jobs, housing, partners etc, and all need our own personal space.

Personal space is just as important in reducing anger, as is the 'space' between stimulus and response. We all like to have our own territory and do feel threatened and angry if that space is invaded. For me my home is my space and entry into that area is by invitation only! It is for me to decide how long any person is allowed to remain within my personal space and I will begin to feel uncomfortable if they overstay their welcome, we are all like this but mostly too polite to deal with it. If I get a situation of the uninvited and unannounced visitor who has taken it upon themselves to burden me with their company just to pass some time, I always feel the stress levels banging on Mr.Angry's door. In this sort of scenario 'Territorial Anger' is only mild but change this slightly to something like coming home to find your house being robbed then a much more serious level of Territorial Anger pops up.

In some parts of the country there are even some pubs and clubs that you cannot go into because the regular inhabitants will make you less than welcome for daring to enter their territory. Even at a football match it could be a bad choice to stand in certain parts of the supporters area if supporters of the opposing team surrounding you.

Territorial aggression can be a very serious thing so never become too complacent about it.

Hostile Aggression has the sole intention of harming another person physically or verbally.

Instrumental Aggression is when something is done with persistence and energy and is a means towards an end. This is done to affect a certain positive outcome such as winning a competition or training event. The Australian football teams are known for performing an aggressive type of ritual dance before a game to try and intimidate the opposing team and to show how strong they are.

Some types of aggression: Predatory, Intermale, Fear induced, Irritable, Territorial, Defensive, Maternal, Instrumental.

Stimulation of the Neural Systems in the Hypothalamus and Limbic System are affected by Hormonal influences, such as the level of testosterone in the blood. Differences in aggression are mainly caused by variation in the sensitivity of these systems and will also change over time depending on the level of hormonal influences within the body.

Intermale Aggression: Between two of the same species.

Stags clash antlers

Men puff out their chests and try to stand taller and broader to appear bigger.

Cats arch up backs and raise fur.

Cowboys flash off their guns in their holsters.

Boxers show off their muscles and build at a weigh in.

Peacocks display their feathers as in a fan shape.

Gorillas beat their chests.

Ice Hockey players barge into each other.

Medical

Damage to the Amygdala has been found to reduce fear-induced aggression in many mammals including man, but it has also been shown that damage to other parts of it can increase irritable aggression. Stimulation of the Amygdala has been reported to produce violent attacks of rage. However in another twist to this, an experiment by Delgado, which took place in 1969, showed that he could stop a raging bull whilst in full charge just by using radio-controlled stimulation of the brain. This has often made me wonder if any of the different types of microwave or radio waves, or even the satellite signals that surround us, have any part in affecting our moods. If you have ever been near to a set of speakers with your mobile phone nearby, you will always know a second or two before your phone rings that you are about to receive a call because the speakers will vibrate with a slight pulsing type noise. Has it ever made you wonder if your brain is also being stimulated by these waves each time we use a mobile phone? I know I do think about that.

Androgen is known to sensitise certain systems within the body effecting aggressive behaviour, as do hormones in adults. Castration effects the reduction of Androgen and is also known to decrease the level if intermale aggression within mammals. This is common practice with dogs. We often have male dogs castrated in an attempt to stop them from being boisterous and aggressive, amongst other things, but from my own experience I know that my former pet Alsatian was still as angry and aggressive after having his castration done. Another medical condition occurs when Lesions of the Amygdala or frontal lobes often do lead to the reduction anger and violence and is also thought to especially effective in reducing fear-induced aggression. However before you rush off to book up your private operation to rid yourself of anger, bear in mind that this is also irreversible and an operation performed to cause this type of change in a person's behaviour can also change their behaviour for the worst! Although this may help to control disturbed individuals who suffer from violent explosive rages, it is not much use in controlling 'normal' learnt aggression.

Empty Heads Have Long Tongues

Some people can really piss you off with their cruel words but they are not always fully aware of what they are saying. They simply do not think before they open their big mouths. I was guilty of this when I used to drink excessive amounts of alcohol and have often ended up fighting with people because I had made them angry with something that I had said. I hadn't intended it that way or meant to be offensive. Alcohol just made me a loudmouth and I shudder at the thought of how I was. But just in the true spirit of 'you're always the last one to know' I couldn't see myself or what a dick-head I was. As I became progressively drunk, my head became emptier and my slurring tongue became bigger. I was an empty head with a long tongue. However I'm not alone in this world. My excuse was that I did not handle my beer too well but there are many individuals out there that can fully charge a long tongue just on the oxygenated blood flowing to their empty head. You are going to have to work out if they are ignorant to what they are saying and are not really being malicious or if they are being nasty. The nasty people I have dealt with elsewhere in the book using methods such as sarcasm so I do not want to repeat it again, here I want to stick to the numbskulls that really haven't a clue what they are doing, due to having nothing between their ears. So are you going to let these ignorant people make you angry? I hope not because it's just like the cat that shits in your garden, it's not personal. The empty head brigade probably doesn't realise that they are rubbing you up the wrong way. They are just too stupid. Stupidness is not a crime- it's a reality and many people suffer from it, so rather than getting angry with them, why not take them to one side and explain the effect that they are having on you. Explain to them that they are not really thinking about what they are saying; Explain to them that now you have made them aware of what they are doing to you, that if it continues to happen it would appear that they are being intentionally malicious towards you.

It may simply be the case that they are just not aware of how other people are seeing them, their actions and how their mouth is letting them down. You are not going to be able to change everybody, just as there are a few things about yourself that others cannot change in you;

but you can at least give it a try. From past experience I have found that a good cure for this is to capture these sort of people on video so that they can take a good look at themselves at a later and more suitable date. Most of us hate hearing our recorded voice on tape when it's played back to us because it's a voice that we do not recognise. Well the same goes for being captured on video, we become even more critical about ourselves especially if caught on camera doing something that we were not aware we were doing. Video is a great reality check for the 'empty head with long tongue brigade' to be brought into touch of how others see them. Although this is a big effort on your part to educate someone as to how ignorant to how they have been acting, it's still much better than getting angry and letting it eat away at you whilst letting them carry on regardless.

If you find that this is not practical and that all your efforts of 'hinting' or speaking to them about their actions are ineffective then you may just have to consider adding them to your list of people that you need to disassociate yourself from in the future.

Ah Ha! Caught You Out!

Nobody likes getting caught out and when they do, embarrassment precedes the second emotion of anger. It may also be the person who is doing the catching out that gets angry rather that the one caught. So lets see some of the scenarios where we have known people to get caught out resulting in someone getting angry!

1. Having an affair 2. Lying 3. Talking about someone 4. Faking illness when they should be at work 5. Sleeping in and being late 6. Secret eating 7. Secret dieting or bulimia 8. Consuming alcohol or drugs and so on. The list goes on forever. Quite simply - nobody likes getting caught out whilst doing something that is wrong or may be regarded by some as being improper. Embarrassment is normally our first emotion, which we sometimes try to disguise by displaying anger because we cannot think quickly of a better way out of an embarrassing situation or a way to explain ourselves.

I remember once overhearing the careless whisper of a good friend to a girl I was dating. That was enough to set off my anger towards the pair of them due to her also being party to the situation rather than an innocent victim. She also became angry with me as her instant cover up and reaction to me having caught her out and her not knowing how else to react. So *'Ah! Caught you out'* also sometimes equals ANGER!

I once had a female friend who was bulimic but in denial about it, however you could not escape the tell tale signs of her breath smelling of sick constantly, due to her forcing herself to be sick all the time. Her problem was that she wanted to stay thin so that she could get a guy to stay with her, wrongly believing that she was fat and is why she couldn't keep a boyfriend long-term.

The truth was that the smell of sick on her breath was the only factor in making guys not want to stay with her. She was a very pretty and slim girl. On one occasion when one of her boyfriends confronted her about her problem after hearing her heaving in the bathroom, she went crazy with anger.

She had been caught out and was embarrassed and enraged by this. With not knowing how to deal with this or how to explain herself, she just responded with anger.

Lets face it! We all know when we are doing something wrong or something that may not be appropriate. So my suggestion is to either don't do it in the first place or prepare your response and justification as to why you did, what you did, rather than exploding in anger just because you don't know what else to do. Also on the other side if it's you that's likely to get angry when you catch someone else out and you have prior knowledge or gut reaction that this is going to happen. Plan your response to this as well so that it is not you getting caught out and being forced to react with anger. Many times when we catch someone out it is due to us having a prior suspicion and anticipate such an event so there is no reason why we cannot work out and rehearse an anger free response!

Through experience of prior situations I have found it to be very common that when anger is displayed unusually and not due to repressed or displaced anger, that you can often see signs of it being used as a panicky cover-up to distract you from what it is that they are really up to. So if you see unusual anger that doesn't appear to have any history or events attached to it then it may be worth putting on the detective hat to see if something crops up that you would not normally have seen. BUT! Don't look for or create something that's not there. Ignore the little voices in your head sometimes because they are not always on your side!

Like Attracts Like!

For me - The opposite of anger is laughter. The reason I say this is because when you are truly angry, your facial muscles and state of mind will not allow you to laugh, yet it will still allow you all your other emotions.

We often hear angry people saying *'don't make me laugh.'* Reason being that anger does not allow true laughter. This is another reason that angry people much prefer to hang about with other angry people whereas happy people attract happy people. Like attracts like!

The sad thing is that angry people will try there hardest to convert others into being angry people as well. This is something quite visible in political and religious anger groups. If you are an angry person you will probably find that you are doing the same thing by trying to convert others into being angry at the same things that you are.

Its time to break the chain between anger and anger! If you find that a Mr. Angry is trying to drag you into his bitter and sad world you may have to consider distancing yourself from them before they poison you into their way of thinking, because they will go on and on until they practically depress you! Either make it clear to them that *'their'* anger is how *'They'* feel and it is not necessarily how you feel towards the subject in question, and that you would prefer not to be dragged into it all. If you find that they are just putting their fingers into their ears and are refusing to listen to you, move on and leave them behind to enjoy their anger on their own.

At least until they are prepared to change or deal with the way that they feel.

If you find that its you that is angry and are trying to drag someone through the doors of your 'anger club', get a grip on yourself and try realise what you are doing before you find that you are the one that's left alone with no one else to talk to!

Take a good look at the angry people that are portrayed on the TV and ask yourself if you really want others to see you in the same way?

Don't Insult my Intelligence

Now here is an area that never fails to create anger. That is when someone insults your intelligence by telling you lies. Its something that never failed to get me angry.

My outlook was that if somebody is lying to me and it is so obvious to anyone that its a lie, then that person must be thinking that I am stupid and naive enough to believe them, then they really are insulting my intelligence.

'Oh I'm sorry I didn't turn up yesterday but I was in the bank when these armed robbers came in and etc etc.'

' I definitely put the money in your letterbox and I'm sure I pushed it all the way in but there was a young lad hanging around watching me so I think he must have......'

'I honestly didn't say that! What I said was...'

'You're only the second bloke I've ever slept with..'

Do you get my drift? It used to really anger me when someone would pull a story straight out from the tall story club and think that I was dim enough to accept it as the truth.

Duh! Overweight I am but stupid I'm not!

We all get angry when were lied to especially when it's a blatant lie. But times have changed and these days I am able to listen to the fable and just smile back as I begin my game of sarcasm to show that I know their game and I am now going to make them work very hard on their story. I will still do it in a way that makes me appear to be naive but will have fun punishing them for telling lies. I wont just be happy for them to say they got a bus. I will also want to know the traffic & weather conditions, how many passengers, the ticket fare, how many stops and so on. By the time I am finished with them they will never want to tell me another lie again.

The game goes something like this.....

'Oh Jamie I'm so sorry that I never got your kids a Xmas pressy. I got caught up at work..blah blah...'

Reply: *'Oh that's alright! The times I've been caught out and found out that a year's notice is not enough in-between each Xmas, its unbelievable isn't it"*

'I tried phoning you three times this week to arrange it with you, its too late now..'

Reply: *'You know what! I'm going to complain to that phone company because I'm paying a lot of money to have caller display on my phone so I know which calls I've missed, yet your number has not come up once alongside all the other missed calls I've had. I want them to check it out because your call might have been an emergency!'*

Can you understand the kind of game I play now?

I don't get angry at the stupidity of people trying to insult my intelligence anymore. I prefer to turn things around and let them feel stupid at even trying to insult my level of understanding and belief in what they are saying. It always works wonderfully and makes them less likely to try bullshitting me again because my game just drains the life out of them. However I still never fail to attract new members of the tall story club at parties and other social events. I seem to attract them like flies. But its fun!

Being lied to is not the only way people can insult your intelligence; how about the rude impatient bossy colleague or boss who talks down to you as if you have no intelligence at all with such comments as,

'Duh! Even a five year old could understand that!'

In my younger days I've made people swallow my fist for talking down to me like that, but its not an option that I'm suggesting you try, after all we are trying to get away from all that anger crap aren't we?

With a boss it is unlikely that you can effectively use the sarcasm approach to dealing with them if you want to remain in employment. So I suggest you use the assertive approach

'Listen, you are bullying and insulting me for trying. I've tried my hardest and I know it may not have performed to your expectations but with more practice and training I can work towards getting there. Please treat me with the equal respect that I give you'

Remember that this is all about ridding you and others of anger, and not about 'keeping your employer happy' so you may find that you have a conflict of emotions within this type of scenario.

Do you get angry when people insult your intelligence?

Jealous Anger

Boy! This is a common one. Feeling angry about someone because we are jealous of them! But even worse is being jealous and being in denial of the fact. The Green-eyed monster 'Jealousy' makes us really nasty and angry at times. I've been there, done it, and wore the T-shirt and have also been victim of it myself and can say with all honesty from both perspectives, it sucks!

It's one of my attributes that I have always hated about myself because it borders on being selfish and I am not a selfish person. Jealousy got a hold of me big-time after I had been cheated on badly twice in a row, which is hard for anybody to deal with. Ex partners you can get over and you even wonder what you ever saw in them in the first place but by getting cheated on it makes you feel like the whole population of the opposite sex (if applicable) are going to do the same to you. It's the wrong outlook to have but whilst I did have it, it was there to stay! The problem here is that the scars that we pick up whilst going through such bad experiences do take a while to heal, if ever, and this can turn us into jealous angry bullies. Yep! That was me. I had it so bad that I intentionally warded off any females that dared even smile at me just incase a relationship formed because I knew how badly I would act towards them due to prior experiences. It would have been the case of 105% of jealous anger for 0% of the female having done nothing wrong. I was completely off my nut and will never allow myself to go down that route again just because of what a couple of bad people did to me in the past. However it's not just relationships that causes jealous anger! Haven't you ever been jealous of somebody who has won millions on the lottery but in your opinion does not deserve it? You think it's you that deserves it, am I right? How about the neighbour that has the flash car or the good job that you also think that you should have? Does it make you jealous and angry?

I get the odd hate mail from Mr.Anonymous telling me that my books are crap and of how he can write much better than me! So why doesn't he sit down and write these books rather than reading my crap books. You see, jealous anger exists everywhere.

In many cases people are jealous but angry at themselves for not attempting to get the things that they want from life. I am often told of how lucky I am in being able to write and sell books. Well I'm sorry matey but its not luck, its bloody hard work with a lot of personal sacrifice in-between. I have written seven books in the last four years and have sat indoors alone probably every Friday and Saturday night throughout this period, working on my books whilst my mates were all out enjoying themselves and chatting up the girls, and they tell me I'm lucky! Yeah right!

I made a lot of sacrifices and still do but I don't know anyone that would give up their weekends out for the next four years to achieve what ever it is that they want in life. Yet people still find it within themselves to get jealous of me!

Take a good look at yourself and see if you are angry because you are Jealous of someone?

The Green-eyed monster is no good to anybody so the sooner you bury it - the better!

Over the years I've found that just as many people who dislike me as like me who read my books and magazine columns just to find something else that they can dislike me for. They scour the magazines and go out of their way to do this, how strange!

You know, when I was daring to enter into the book writing world and scribe my first book, it looked to me that the marketplace was fairly saturated with martial art publications, with most of these by my mate Geoff Thompson, yet that did not deter me. I knew that it would be very hard for me to break through because people would draw many similar parallels to Geoff and me and that they would ignore our points of difference and just disregard me if I let them. I could have just sat back and looked on with jealous anger because Geoff had done something that I wanted to achieve myself, but could not now do this, because I had been beaten to pole position. But no! I knew that we had points of difference and that I had to use this to break through and write that book I always dreamed about. I decided to write from the heart and with passion about self-protection from my perspective. Seven books later I have made my mark and have even made my pal Geoff proud of my achievements. However lurking in the shadows I also had another friend who became a tad jealous when I told him that I was considering writing my first book. He replied by telling me that I would never sell a single copy but he was also writing a book, which would take the world by storm! His idea was unrelated to the audience that I was writing for but it was a good idea and he could have made a success of it. It was not a subject that I would want to be associated with but I would still have helped him to get his book out as I do with many other people now. Anyway instead of him sitting down and working hard on his idea so that he could get it into print. He preferred to waste his time and energy in scouring the magazines for reviews that were published about my book or me.

He wasted so much time being jealous and angry that it even stopped him from being my friend. He found it hard to be genuinely pleased for all I had achieved! The moral here is that you will deteriate and waste away if you let jealous anger get a grip of you. Try to recognise it within yourself and deal with it rather than wasting your life worrying about what other people are doing!

Is Your Anger Justified?

We have already covered this within many different places in this book and here we have it again with a heading all of its own just incase you missed it! So is your anger justified?

Are you giving a 105% reaction to a situation that put into perspective is only deserving of 5% worth of anger?

Is it displaced and repressed anger that you have picked up on your journey throughout the day or even throughout your life that you have unleashed on some poor soul? Do you recognise any of this?

How about

'Today is not a good day for anybody to piss me off'

To me, this indicates that you may be carrying say 90% worth of anger before you even come into contact with the next unexpecting victim who may just slightly rub you up the wrong way.

I've seen many situations where such minor incidents have been dealt with 105% worth of anger due to that person already being supercharged with anger. I've done it myself when a string of incidents beyond my control has had a progressive build up within my proverbial pressure cooker and I've blown my top at a harmless minor incident. I've seen many stressed adults do this with their own children after a hard day at work. There are many things that will continue to anger you in life but if you were really honest with yourself you would see that they are really minor events and only deserve minor response if any response at all. If you try to deal with a situation that warrants only 5% of your anger whilst you are fully charged with 105% of built up anger, how do you ever expect to diffuse it or bring it down to a manageable level when you cannot even bring yourself down a level?

Try to take each situation that causes your anger and treat it as a lone event on its own merit. You may just find that your anger is not justified at all.

Why Treat Anger?

The answer is quite simple. If you don't, you will make yourself ill, depressed, sad, and hurt, both physically and mentally. The physical aspect may be that you get into a physical encounter and get hurt or you may get so uptight and depressed that you self-harm or even attempt suicide!

That alone is a good enough reason why you should treat your anger. Bad anger is just no good for you and does nothing positive for your well-being.

In the song 'Stan' by rap artist Eminem it tells the story of a fan who built up anger within himself because he wrote to his idol and did not receive a reply, falsely believing that the star was ignoring him. This was not true and just something the fan had created in his own mind. The idol was just busy and took a while to reply to all his fan mail but by the time he did reply to the fan, he had killed himself, his girlfriend and their unborn child in a car suicide.

Many people let anger get a grip of them in the same way and can end up harming themselves or others. This is why you must treat your anger. If you don't, the hungry wolves will snap at you one by one until you are drained and cannot fight back any more, then when anger has eaten up all your energy; you will be easy prey for the scavenging vultures who will take what's left of you. Unless you can make your anger 'good anger' which you can use in a positive way to get yourself out of a dangerous situation, you must do all you can to rid yourself of it before it drags you down faster than you will ever realise.

From now on, instead of asking yourself *'why treat anger?'* you should be asking yourself *'How to treat anger?'* and that is something that this book will help you explore.

Another thing to consider is that if you do not treat your anger, you will begin to lose people around you, be it colleagues, friends or family. People cannot be bothered having angry people around them. Nobody wants to be dragged down to the land of bitterness and anger with you. If you choose to take that route then you will only find yourself at the end of your journey. You have been warned so don't look back in anger and wonder where it all went wrong.

Predicting Anger

We are very good at predicting when we think a situation involving anger is about to happen. People watching is pretty easy when it comes to spotting someone who is about to explode into an angry rage. Our perception causes our reaction, and the way that we perceive that somebody is going to react, or how we perceive the outcome of a confrontation is going to be, is very important to us!

Young people for instance are often given a clue that some form of violence is on its way by little clues given to then such as; *'You wait till your father gets home, he's going to be very angry with you and will give you a good hiding.'*

Predicting anger is a great ability to have because it can help you to avoid or defuse a situation before it happens. The child for example has the rest of the day to make amends before the father gets home to defuse the situation. Even if you are not on the receiving end of anger and it is your own anger that you are predicting, you can predict its estimated time of arrival and then do all you can to stop it happening. This is why predicting anger is so important to you.

Of all the years that I spent as a doorman or within the security field, the one thing that I always prided myself on was my ability to scan a nightclub or pub with my eyes and predict where situations were becoming a little heated and are likely to develop into anger and violence. This prediction always allowed me to intervene and stop a situation progressing into something more uncontrollable. It is at times like this when prevention is much better than a cure.

In relationships there are many times when one partner is able to recognise within the other, repeated actions that they know will follow up with abuse or violence, sometimes heightened by drugs or alcohol. My initial advice to those in such environments and relationships is to get out because its rare for these violent abusive types to change, at least whilst they are being allowed to carry on like this. I do realize however that many people are too frightened to break free from these abusive relationships and feel they do not have a better alternative so carry on accepting the abuse.

Some even sadly come from the school of thought *'better the devil that you know'* but my school of thought is that if you stay with a wanker, you will always be treated like one. My own mother was one such person who felt *'better the devil you know'* and I watched her take years of abuse as I grew up. It goes against the grain for me to tell you to pacify your abuser as much as possible to keep yourself from harm, but if you are not prepared to escape an abusive relationship then that's all I can do!

If you predict that anger is about to pay you a visit, do all you can to keep it at bay. It's hard to advise you to not fight back but avoidance is a valid response to dealing with anger, especially if you are not going to get out of an abusive relationship. If you are not going to get out then you will have to make the best of a bad thing. Anger is ugly but violence is even worse, so if you can predict it's about to happen then you must try deal with it at a simple level and try to defuse it. Even as I write I can feel the tenseness and tightness of my clenched teeth and jaw just thinking about the violence and abuse that some men throw at women and children. It sickens me!

Another thing to think about with predicting anger is that it's so strange that when we know that coming into contact with certain people will make them or us angry, yet we still enter into environments where we know this is likely to happen. Some are unavoidable but not all. If you know that going to the local pub or club is going to anger you when you see your former partner with someone new, don't go there. Find something else to do. You are already predicting what is going to happen with your feelings so why not avoid it and prevent it happening. Just go to the cinema instead or treat yourself to the company of someone that will make you feel good. Can you predict what will happen if you step into a lions cage? How about if you stepped off a fast moving bus? Or if you dive into a pool with out water? We can pretty much predict what the outcomes will be so we avoid such things, so the same should apply to Anger. We can guess where things are headed when predicting someone's behaviour is going to lead to anger towards us, so we must also avoid such scenarios and situations. Predict Anger and Avoid it!

The Interview

Every time we encounter someone and engage in conversation, an interview begins and it is a two-way thing! This is also the beginning of a grooming process for many people. Whether you realise it or not, that's exactly what is happening. Conversation does not even have to take place because the interview begins mostly with eye contact apart from that which is done over the phone, text messages, email, letters etc. Normally though it is the eye contact that usually determines as to whether we want to further engage into conversation wit someone.

Although 'the interview' is important to us when striking up new relationships, it is also important where it may possibly allow you to detect an argument or situation that may lead on to violence. It is at the time of the interview that we need to diffuse someone who is angry with us.

Detecting Anger within an interview is something that we all have experience in - we do not need help or training within this department! The only thing that many of us may be unaware of is the fact that we are experiencing an actual interview as opposed to it just being unimportant small talk as we may have regarded it to be before.

Every encounter is an interview of sort. Most of them are quite innocent and good willed conversations but others can be calculated and harmful. If you are finding it hard to get to grips with the term 'interview' then just change it to the word 'conversation' but just remind yourself when you need to that you are still being interviewed, and that someone is trying to suss you out or you them. So to all intents and purposes it really is an interview.

We use it when chatting someone up, when buying or selling a car, or in any sort of exchange and it is a tool of the trade for bullies or criminals.

I am a very hard person to interview because I am fully aware of how the game works and know when somebody is trying to play the game with me. I will recognise that you are interviewing me even if you don't realise it yourself, that you are doing so.

Some people are very amateurish and bad at concealing the fact that they are trying to obtain information from you, whereas others are real experts at it. My main reason for including the interview section within this book is because hidden beneath the surface of many interviews sits 'Anger'. Here is an example of some unfriendly beginnings to interviews that you may recognise;

'Is that your car parked across my drive?' = I am Angry!

'What you looking at?' = I am Angry!

With all these interview questions, the angry interviewee is just dying for you to reinforce and justify their anger by giving them certain reply.

I.e. *'Yes that is my car, I'm sorry'* or *'Sorry, I wasn't talking to you'*, or even *'Sorry, I wasn't looking at you.'* In all these cases you are apologising to avoid an argument but without realising it your apology may be adding fuel to the fire of anger. It is at this stage that you need to act quickly without delay by acting or replying in a way that will put out the anger flame rather than fuelling it.

You can still be apologetic without appearing weak or afraid. You can answer in a way that will show that you realise you have upset someone but without appearing to give an apology that may show you as weak. I'm not saying here that its wrong to apologise because it's not, rather I am giving you ideas as to not let the angry person think you are weak enough to be bullied. Some bullies do take apologies as being a sign of weakness.

Here is a play on word's to give you an idea of what I'm talking about.

'I can see I've upset you. It was unintentional and I will resolve that right now and remove my car. I made a mistake without realizing and will make sure it doesn't happen again'

Or

'I wasn't talking to you but can I be of any help?'

Or

'I was looking to see if anyone had a watch on because I need to know the time'

All we are doing here is backing off from a situation, which is not the same as backing down.

If you could just take a few minutes out of each day as if they never happened, you will have a much anger free life if those few minutes were to contain some type of heated exchange. Don't get drawn into the angry interview, its just not worth it. Just recognise it for all its worth and go about your business without being dragged into the clever interview where you may end up harmed.

Pass the anger interview by, like a ship passing in the night.

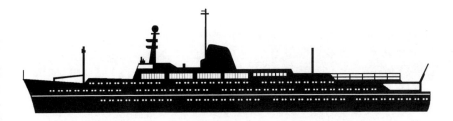

Anger at Death

Here is a subject that will affect us all at sometime in our lives, that being exposure to death. Many people experience a big difference in the way that they think and what is now of importance to them when suddenly faced with a life-threatening crisis. Their priorities begin to change just as if a long-term relationship with a partner is about to end or reorganisation of life is about to begin.

Death is something very hard to deal with and come to terms with. I can remember being angry at the death of a young child some years back after hearing on the news that he was out buying a mothers day present when a bomb exploded in the high street, planted by some terrorist group. I did not know the boy or even anyone that knew him but the taking of an innocent youngster's life, aged around six years old really made me feel angry. It was a senseless killing. I do not follow sport, politics or religion so was not able to accept any justification from anybody as to why it was this young lad's time to die.

Although many other children have been killed in similar and even worse circumstances than this, I still remember clearly to this day how saddened and angry it made me feel that this lad's life was taken.

Even when my own parents died I did not feel anger at their death. I was devastated and upset beyond belief but do not remember anger at it being their time to go.

I know that many people are angered by death for many different reasons so I would like to cover this area.

My mother died whilst I was writing this book and this made me just shut myself away from the rest of the world. While alone and feeling sad and sorry for myself I decided to write down everything that I could about the way I felt and created a list of all the feelings and emotions that I was going through. This I did over a two-week period whilst I was dealing with the aftermath of the bereavement.

Some of the words I jotted down were:

Anger, Death, Taken away, Out of control, Breakdown, Abandonment, Emptiness, Rejection, Loneliness, Frustration, Divorce, Tiredness, Sadness, Low esteem, Blame, Forsaken, Confusion, Helpliness, Low confidence, Neglect, Despair, Grief, Shock, Numbness, Disbelief, Reorganisation of life.

Although I did not feel anger at my mother's death, I felt anger towards others. I felt angry towards all the people that had treated her badly. I felt angry that she had killed herself with alcohol even though informed by specialists that she would die if she carried on drinking, when they last saved her life. Also I was angry with other people at not being as sad as me about my mother dying. I was especially angry at some of the comments that were thoughtlessly put to me such as 'Well at least your mother has gone to a better place'. Well excuse me, but if it is such a better place then why are we all not packing our bags and making the same journey? What are we still doing here? I know that my outlook is a little different to most people based on the fact that I don't have religion or spirituality in my life, but I do have commonsense, and that tells me that if we were given the choice and option to take ourselves and our families to a better place than we have now, we would do it, wouldn't we? After all isn't that why we go on holidays. So the 'better place' argument relating to death does not cut any ice with me. It just makes me feel angry at people's ignorance or their insult to my intelligence. However as time has passed I have come to realise that on different times of the day and on different days, I would be suffering from one of many different emotions that I wrote on my list and this in turn would affect how I reacted and felt towards other people. The more I thought about it, the more I realised that people just didn't know what to say or how to react around someone who has suffered a loss such as a bereavement. It's really no fault of theirs.

I think that my main problem was that whenever anybody ever mentioned my mother to me, all I could see was my last ever vision of her in hospital as she died and it was not a pleasant memory. In fact it was horrible and I will never forget the life pulse beating away on the hospital monitor and beginning to skip beats and become irregular until it finally stopped. That moment I knew that there was no possibility that I will ever be able to hear my mother's voice, or see her smile ever again. She had blood coming from her eye, nose and mouth and tubes inserted into her body. This is the picture of my mother that I see when her name is ever mentioned to me, as it probably is to the other family around her deathbed. But this is not what others see when they mention her. They remember how they last saw her, which would be laughing, joking, smiling, drinking and being caring. They have a pleasurable memory that I am not yet able to share. They cannot see through my eyes and have not had my experience, so naturally they are not going to feel as upset as I did when her name was mentioned. Result being that I was getting angry at others not feeling as sad as I did, but I understand all that now. My whole point to mention my own experience is not for self pity because that's not my style, but rather because you will one day have a similar experience to mine if you haven't already, and you also will feel anger with others for not feeling as sad as you do. However you must realise that you cannot expect others to go through the grieving process for you. It is your loss and you are going to have to work through it yourself without expecting others to feel your pain for you. Feelings of anger and sadness are normal when you have suffered a loss. I even felt angry at myself at one stage because I felt that I should have been more upset than I actually was!

Don't get me wrong, I broke down in tears whilst in denial that she was laying in front of me dead, whilst being comforted by the nurses, doctors, and my family in the ward, but a week later I still felt that I was not as upset as I wanted or expected to be!

I felt that something was wrong with me, and that made me feel guilty. It took a while for the penny to drop before I realised that I had actually been in mourning for years without even realizing it. For over 25 years I had seen my mother put another nail in her coffin each time that she attempted suicide or was hospitalised due to her alcohol abuse killing off her body. I had been in **'Anticipitationary mourning'** for over two decades because I had already lost the sober healthy mother that I once remembered as a child. It was like knowing two different people and watching the 'Alcohol induced' mother gradually possessing and taking over the mind and body of my real mother, more and more each day. It was only after thinking long and hard about this that I was able to stop being angry with myself for not being more upset than I thought I should be. Another thing that this made me realise is that people also go through a similar gut wrenching feeling when they break up or lose a partner for a multitude of reasons. For me it is very similar to experiencing death because I refuse to let myself remain in contact with former partners. I treat it just like a death and reorganise my life just as I had to when my mother died. This is what works for me and allows me to go forward in my life and also removes the possibility of me ever getting back with someone. Just like a shark who cannot swim backwards, I refuse to let myself go backwards in life and this is what works best for me. I wont even have former partners in my life as friends! That's just me and how I deal with this type of grieving. I relate it as closely as I can to grieving over a death. I'm not saying that this is the best way for you, its just what works for me but has also denied me investing any emotional energy in the future possibilities of relationships as avoidance is easier for me to deal with than grieving a loss.

So have a good think about what I've said on Anger at Death, be it your own suffering or that of a friend or acquaintance because nothing can be more final than death, which is a shock to all of us when it comes.

The reorganisation of our lives whether it is a death mourning or relationship break-up mourning, will constantly remind us of any loss that we have suffered. It may change out lives completely and is a change that will be frightening at first but will make us stronger and more prepared if we were to suffer another kind of loss in the future.

Another thing to consider here also is how anger may evolve when another person attempts to bring you into a premature acceptance of your loss.

Acceptance takes time, but time takes time, and this will be different for everyone. Remember that we only ever see the outer shell of people and can never truly know how they are feeling inside.

After the murder of his schoolboy son, unrelated to the earlier death I mentioned, Colin Cokes said of his son's killers *'We do not feel anger towards them - we feel sorrow for what has happened to them and our son'* (Daily Star 25th March 2000).

Some people will even begin to act differently, even strangely after bereavement, it's quite common but something that may make them angry if you make an unnecessary fuss about it. This was what happened to me:

I have been an avid tea drinker for around 30 years and would drink about 20 mugs of tea per day. Even when I became a non-meat eater and stopped drinking milk around 8 years ago, I could not give up my tea so I used Soya milk. I just loved tea!

However from the day my mother died, I never drank another cup of tea again. I began drinking cans of sugar free cola which is something I never liked and also gave up regular consumption of alcohol.

When I analysed this behaviour some months later, wondering why I could still not drink tea, I realised that having a cup of tea was a ritual that I would always go through when ever I visited my mother. Every week without fail I would visit her and give her as much money as she needed and take bags of shopping around for her. Whilst I was there she would make us both a cup of tea, which was her attempt to disguise the fact that she had been drinking alcohol that day. She knew that I did not approve of her drinking, so she would make the effort for the time of my visit. We take on many of our parent attributes without even realizing it and tea drinking was one of my mothers that I took on from when I was young. When my mother died and no longer able to drink tea, I also strangely stopped drinking tea.

I put my tea drinking to rest when I laid my mother to rest. That's the only explanation I can come up with. To this day I have never touched another cup of tea after 30 constant years of drinking it.

I also think that the drinking of sugar free cola is connected too because it was the only drink available throughout my stay at my mother's bedside from the machine!

My whole point here is that you may notice some strange or unusual behaviour within someone who has suffered a loss. If they are not at risk of harming themselves or others then let them be, because if you try to force different behaviour within them you may also induce anger. They are most likely displaying behaviour connected or related to the person that they have lost so there is no need to rush out and buy a straight jacket for them.

Don't try to challenge or change their behaviour if it is harmless because we each need to grieve in our own way. I do hope this section on anger at death has made you at least look at things a little differently on how death and anger are related because there will be a period in your life when you have to experience this.

You're Scared of Him Aren't You?

Those cutting words from a partner saying *'You're scared of him (or her) aren't you?'* are no stranger to our ears, are they? And isn't it oh so easy to reply with *'Ok I will show you who is scared, just watch what I can do.'*

Are you really stupid enough to fall for the oldest power and control trick in the world by reacting to a few words like that?

It's no fun being in this situation and it tears your stomach out because you will feel that you need to prove yourself but don't get sucked in by this bullshit. If you come over to me and tell me I'm a fat bastard, I have two choices. I can push my fingers deep into your eye sockets, or I allow you to have your say. It is my choice to allow you to have the last word. It is my choice to allow you to call me a name, and it is also my choice if I want to blind you or bite out your windpipe. You are not calling the shots, I am! Whatever way you want to play the game, you are still not going to be in control of me, I'm going to be the one in control over my actions because I will decide if either of us will leave this encounter in an ambulance, police car, hearse, or we both walk away unscathed. I'm in control so much here that I may even allow you to have the final word and still allow you to walk away. This is nothing to do with being scared; it's about being in control of our own actions and reactions rather than allowing someone else to do it for us.

It's quite funny when people don't get you to react in the way that they want you to do. They get freaked out and just don't know what to do next. They become confused because you won't play their game. Let me give you an example of something that happened to me a few years ago. I had parked my car in an awkward spot whilst I was waiting for a former girlfriend to return from a shop. In doing so I had caused a problem for oncoming vehicles to get past me and I was not able to reverse. By the time she had returned I had managed to piss a few people off due to my inconsiderate parking.

I was now stuck and could neither go forward or backwards, forcing a van to squeeze by me. As it did the driver unwound his window and screamed out *' Are you fucking stupid or what, parking like a prat?'* Bah Blah Blah!!! As this is all going on I looked into his cab and saw a young lad around 10 years olds shaking with fear in anticipation of what was going to happen next, due to his father's threatening behaviour. I could see the poor lad trying not to make eye contact with me and had probably seen this scenario with his father a hundred times before. At that time in my life, had the anger bully been alone I have no doubt that I would have pulled him through the open window and gone a few rounds with him for gobbing off to me in front of my former partner. But never with a child present. On this particular day I just looked at him and let him on his way. It was nothing to do with this book because it wasn't written then. It was purely down to the fact of a young child being present. Shortly after the guy had gone I heard the cutting female voice *'You're scared of him aren't you? I cant believe that you didn't get out and beat him up, why did you let him get away with that?'* She actually expected me to use physical violence for a stupid unimportant event that lasted about five seconds. I shook my head in disbelief in what I was hearing from her mouth and replied *'Violence is not the answer to everything you know, that guy doesn't even know me and as for that poor little kid'* She snapped back with *'So what are you a fucking bouncer turned hippy?'*

She was actually trying to bully me into going after the guy and beating his brains in. She was a very angry person. Angry at the world and trying to use me to unleash her anger. This is a girl who tried her hardest to get me to kill someone for her and attempted suicide because I wouldn't. I sure attract them. Anyway getting back to the road rage story, can you see how easy it would be to fall into that trap of letting another person control you with the classic *'you're scared of him aren't you.'* If you are ever in the situation of an angry partner trying that cutting line on you, don't fall for it. Some people are very good at passing their anger on to you in this way and for a few seconds that an incident may last, its just not worth the change that it could make to your life or another's. You are in control of yourself and you must be the one that decides how that unimportant few seconds will affect the rest of your life. In my particular situation, the only one scared was a poor frightened young boy.

Conclusion

When I began writing my first book *'Dogs don't know kung fu'* on the subject of female Self-protection, I was a very angry person. Angry at the abuse that females suffer from males, angry at how this abuse touched on my own family, angry at the world because harm and suffering was still going on within the lives of so many people, many that I knew but many more that I didn't know.

I was pretty much angered by everything and anything that I came into contact with. I did not recognise my anger as such because I didn't remember life as being any different. From being a young child all I knew was the feeling of being angry. It has taken about thirty years for me to come to terms and recognise that I have been giving a free ride to the emotion of anger in many shapes and forms and it had now become time to shake off this freeloader.

I had to take an in-depth look at the human emotion of anger in order to understand as much as I possibly could about it, in order for me to deal with it. There was a lot to digest and most of it self-revealing and a bitter pill to swallow. I did a lot of reflecting on my past behaviour.

What I have learnt along the way is that there are millions of different excuses that we give ourselves as to why we are angry with a person or a situation but when you analyse the true reason for your anger, you are more likely going to find that just one event or experience in your life, has caused a long term suppressed anger which in turn causes you to lead an angry life. Not always though because some new things will always crop up and anger us if we let them.

I personally wasted three decades living my life like this and would have continued to see out the rest of my days doing things the way that my suppressed anger would let me. I would have carried on reacting, responding, communicating, and dealing with people at a level that my anger would allow me to.

It has taken this book to break me free from this mould and I am certain that without all the research that I have gone through and the analytical approach I took with the whole concept of anger, I would still be giving a free ride to anger.

I do not believe that there is just one method or way of dealing with your anger or somebody else's anger, because it rears it's head in many different shapes and forms, however I do believe that now you have read this book, you will be able to deal, manage or eradicate anger so that you can benefit with a more fruitful life. You will now be able to recognise anger within yourself and within others in a way that you have never seen it before. You will also understand how easy it is for people to press each other's anger buttons and that you do react in a habitual manner when angry with others as they do you.

If nothing else, I will have made you think more about the subject of anger which will now allow you to deal with future situations from a more informed choice, allowing various reactional options rather than how habit has forced you to act in the past. I could have carried on writing forever about anger because it is not an area that you can comprehensively squeeze into a small book like this, however I have now given you the tip of the iceberg. You can now look further into the subject for areas that will aid you further in analysing and dealing with your particular form of anger or that of someone who is angry with you. Don't let anger make you as ill as it did me, both physically and even worse, mentally.

I personally have had some good people come into my life and jump straight back out on the next available train due to my anger. I have also played an important part in other people's lives who have forced me into choosing a future without them due to their anger and how it has allowed or forced them to act.

I no longer want anger in my life or angry people in my life, so with the help of this book and a lot of perseverance, I will do all I can to help others to rid themselves of anger.

Now you have read this book you will no doubt have learnt something about anger that you were unaware of before and will be thinking to yourself

'I could have discovered this information by reading just a page or two from this book and did not need to read the rest'

Well sure you could if you knew what it was in the first place that you didn't know. But the point is that much of the information in the book is pretty much the same or cross-referenced because all of the attributes that are part of angers makeup, are all interlinked.

I also believe that just because you were able to learn and absorb something new just from a few particular pages, it does not mean that everybody else understands the message in the same way; they may need to hear it from a different angle in order to understand more about anger. They will also be able to claim that all they needed to know was contained within just a few pages, but their few pages may not be the same as your few pages. So the book has been padded out with underpinning knowledge (over 62,000 words worth) so as to help the majority rather than the chosen few. If nothing else, I hope I hope that my existence has had a positive effect in educating, creating, motivating or making a difference to somebody's life and I hope they in turn will do the same for others and so on to the next generation. I want my life to have been worthwhile to me, and others I come into contact with. If I have made you think differently about anything in life in a positive way then I have been successful.

Please try some of the things in this book for yourself and on others that you care for and remember that you will have to spend some time working on it. It took me about two years to rid myself of 30 years of anger. Time takes time.

I hope with the help of this book that you can free yourself and others from that emotion that we know as anger until of course, its needed for your own safety.

Best of luck

Jamie
March 2001

THUGS MUGS AND VIOLENCE

Want to know what its like
when it really kicks off?

Forget the movies - this is the REAL world.

Jamie O'Keefe

www.newbreedbooks.co.uk

THUGS, MUGS
and
VIOLENCE
REVIEWED AS
'BOOK OF THE MONTH'
Front magazine

£ 14 inc p&p
from
NEW BREED
Po box 511, Dagenham Essex RM9 5DN

 Reg Kray telephoned me from prison, after having just undergone eye surgery to talk through the foreword for the re-print of this book.

Due to time restraints and the restrictions that he is bound by, I asked him if he could sum up his thoughts, on this book in a lone paragraph, rather than a lengthy foreword. Although Reg has given me his consent to quote him in length on all the good things that he has said about this book. I have decided to just go with the lone paragraph which was written by Reg himself. *'Thugs mugs and violence'* now has a permanent place within the cell of Reg Kray and is also read by the other inmates.

Thank you Reg for you phone-calls, sometimes three a day, to share your thoughts, ideas, opinions and philosophies with me.

Your friend
Jamie

'Jamie's book 'Thugs, Mugs and Violence' is an insight into the violent times of today and should be read' **Reg Kray – Kray Twins**

Photograph kindly supplied to me
for inclusion
by Reg Kray

REG KRAY – 32 YEARS SERVED

1968 – 2000 HM Prison. R.I.P.

A MUST FOR ALL FEMALES

PREVENT YOURSELF FROM BECOMING A VICTIM
'Dogs don't know Kung Fu'
A guide to Female Self Protection
By Jamie O'Keefe **£14** including post & packing
Never before has Female Self Protection used this innovative approach to pose questions like. Why do Rapist's Rape? Why are Women abused? Why do Stalkers Stalk? This book takes a look at all Simple, Serious, and Life threatening aspects of Self Protection that concern us daily, along with **PREVENTION** of Child abuse and Child Abduction, Emotional cruelty, Telephone abuse, Road rage, Muggers, Date rape, Weapon attacks, Female abduction, Sexual Assault & Rape, Self defence law, and what it will allow us to do to protect ourselves, plus much more. With over 46,500 words, 77 pictures and 200 printed pages 'Dog's Don't Know Kung fu' is a no nonsense approach to women's self defence. It covers many realistic scenarios involving Children's abduction as well as typical attacks on women. Besides quoting actual events, the book explains how to avoid trouble and how you should react if you get into a situation.

This book is a 'must read' for all women and parents.
It is also important for teenage women, but, due to some of its graphic depiction's of certain incidences, parents should read it first and decide if it's suitable for their child.

In Your Face
'CLOSE QUARTER FIGHTING'
by
Kevin O'Hagan

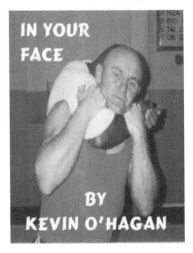

£14

from

NEW BREED

Your Advert, Book, Video or Company could be featured here
plus in our other books

What makes tough guys tough?
The Secret Domain

WHAT MAKES

TOUGH GUYS
TOUGH
The Secret Domain
by Jamie O'Keefe

Written by Jamie O'Keefe

Jamie O'Keefe has interviewed key figures from boxing, martial arts, self-protection, bodyguards, doorwork, military, streetfighting and so on. Asking questions that others were too polite to ask but secretly wanted to know the answers.

Interviews include **Peter Consterdine, Geoff Thompson,** and **Dave Turton** from the countries leading self-protection organisations 'The British Combat Association' and the 'Self Defence Federation.'

Along with Boxing heroes **Dave 'Boy' Green** and East London's former Commonwealth Champion '**Mo Hussein.**'

Plus unsung heroes from the world of Bouncers, Foreign Legion, Streetfighters, and more.

This book also exposes the Secret Domain, which answers the question 'What makes tough guys tough.'

Find out what some of the toughest guys on the planet have to say about 'What makes tough guys tough' and how they would turn you into a tough guy.

Available from NEW BREED at £14 inc p&p

How would you like to be able to
Stop an attack in its tracks?

How would you also like to be able to do it
within a second or two?

How would you like to do it without even
having to draw a breath?

Finally, would you like to know what the
alternative to grappling is?

Then get

'Pre-emptive strikes for winning fights'
'The alternative to grappling'

by
Jamie O'Keefe

Pre-emptive strikes
for winning fights
'The alternative to grappling'

by
Jamie O'Keefe
£14 inc P&P
from
New Breed
Po Box 511
Dagenham, Essex RM9 5DN

Combat
Magazine

Self Protection Column in
each issue by
Jamie O'Keefe
Available from
Temple Publishing
Tel: 0121 3443737
And all newsagents